Praise for
The Unofficial Disney Parks Holidays Cookbook

"Ashley has truly made it possible to experience the magic of a Disney holiday right in your own kitchen! Having the recipes for so many crowd-favorite snacks (I'm looking at you, Mickey Gingerbread!) is such a gift, and a must for any Disney Parks foodie!"

—**MEG DILEO**, *Magic with Meg*

"This cookbook is perfect for any Disney fan who loves the holidays! *The Unofficial Disney Parks Holidays Cookbook* brings the spirit of the Disney holiday treats to you—and helps create special moments at home!"

—**DIANA HUGHES**, *Being Mommy with Style*

"Ashley has done it again! There is no place like Disney for the holidays, and thanks to *The Unofficial Disney Parks Holidays Cookbook*, everyone can experience Disney holiday magic at home! What better way to bring people together during the holidays than a shared love of Disney food?"

—**SARAH LEMP**, *Motor City Mouse*

"Our family loves using Ashley's cookbooks for re-creating the indulgent treats from our favorite Disney trips. I can't wait to add these seasonal offerings to that lineup as well!"

—**ALYSSA STANDER**, *Lemon Drop Travels*

"There's nothing we love more than bringing the magic of our vacation home with us, and being able to bake together is a chance to build on those memories we made and let them grow—even after we're home."

—**REBECCA SCHLER**, *Miracles on Main Street*

"Ashley and her Disney cookbooks bring the magic and tastes of the Disney Parks into our home. Disney feels extra magical around the holidays, so this just seems perfect to add to my collection!"

—**KARYN ORMSTON**, *@awesomemagicfam*

"There is something for everyone in this cookbook. Salty, spicy, sweet, savory, and everything in between. These easy-to-follow recipes will give your heart and tummy a great big Wookiee hug (the best) and transport you back to the most magical place on Earth."

—**SADIE FOURNIER**, *former Star Wars: Galactic Starcruiser Cast Member*

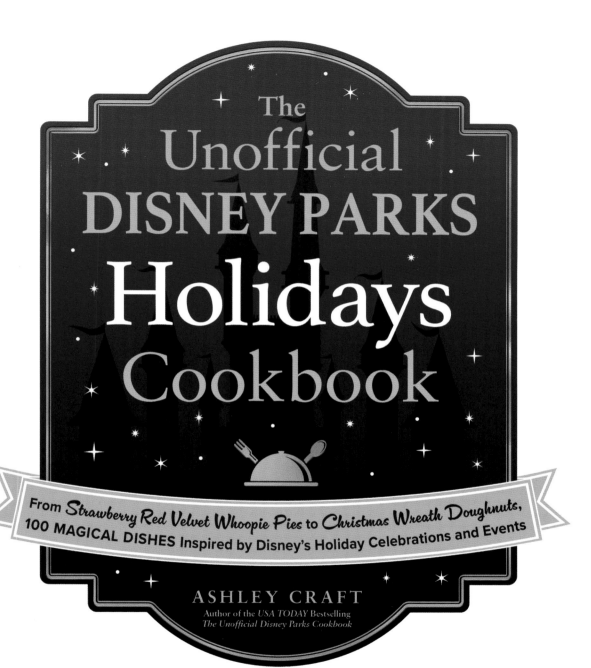

The Unofficial DISNEY PARKS Holidays Cookbook

From *Strawberry Red Velvet Whoopie Pies* to *Christmas Wreath Doughnuts,* 100 MAGICAL DISHES Inspired by Disney's Holiday Celebrations and Events

ASHLEY CRAFT

Author of the *USA TODAY* Bestselling
The Unofficial Disney Parks Cookbook

ADAMS MEDIA
NEW YORK LONDON TORONTO SYDNEY NEW DELHI

Adams Media
An Imprint of Simon & Schuster, LLC
100 Technology Center Drive
Stoughton, Massachusetts 02072

First Adams Media hardcover edition September 2024

ADAMS MEDIA and colophon are registered trademarks of Simon & Schuster, LLC.

Simon & Schuster: Celebrating 100 Years of Publishing in 2024

For information about special discounts for bulk purchases, please contact Simon & Schuster Special Sales at 1-866-506-1949 or business@simonandschuster.com.

The Simon & Schuster Speakers Bureau can bring authors to your live event. For more information or to book an event, contact the Simon & Schuster Speakers Bureau at 1-866-248-3049 or visit our website at www.simonspeakers.com.

Interior design by Sylvia McArdle
Photographs by Harper Point Photography
Photography chefs: Martine English, Christine Tarango, Kira Friedman
Interior maps and illustrations by Alaya Howard and Russell Tate; © 123RF

Manufactured in the United States of America

10 9 8 7 6 5 4 3 2

Library of Congress Cataloging-in-Publication Data
Names: Craft, Ashley, author.
Title: The unofficial Disney Parks Holidays cookbook / Ashley Craft, Author of the USA TODAY Bestselling The Unofficial Disney Parks Cookbook.
Description: First Adams Media hardcover edition. | Stoughton, Massachusetts: Adams Media, [2024] | Series: Unofficial cookbook gift series | Includes index.
Identifiers: LCCN 2024013272 | ISBN 9781507220337 (hc) | ISBN 9781507220344 (ebook)
Subjects: LCSH: International cooking--California--Disneyland. | Disneyland (Calif.) | LCGFT: Cookbooks.
Classification: LCC TX725.A1 C639 2024 | DDC 641.5/68--dc23/eng/20240327
LC record available at https://lccn.loc.gov/2024013272

ISBN 978-1-5072-2033-7
ISBN 978-1-5072-2034-4 (ebook)

Dedication

To my good friends Haley Hemphill and Ariel Letts.
You add magic to my life!

Contents

CHAPTER 4

Magic Kingdom. . . 73

CHAPTER 5

EPCOT. . . 99

Acknowledgments

As always, my number one thanks goes to my husband, Danny. He is my biggest fan and brightens every day of my life. Love you, Danny! Thanks for being you.

Special thanks to my research assistants for this book. The book was a *long* time in the making, so there are a lot of them: Ariel Letts and Haley Hemphill came along for Disneyland Halloween *twice* (and Ariel a third time in the spring!) and helped with a lot of ideas for this book. I'm so grateful to them for their friendship and for always being on call! My sister-in-law and I dressed up as Wall-e and Eva for Walt Disney World Halloween, so thanks, Kacey Ableman, for going along with my antics. Kara Boucher researched holidays at Walt Disney World with me even though she was pregnant, so thank you! My mother, Karen Peterson, came with me to Walt Disney World in the spring for some research and to support my speaking at a conference; thanks, Mom, for always being by my side and rallying behind me! My friend AnnaMarie Ferrell and her boys, Aiden and Jack, helped taste-test some summertime snacks, so thanks for giving up some of your summer vacation to do that! And lastly, my daughter, Hazel, got to come along for a mommy-and-me trip in November to wrap up our final taste-testing trip; it was so fun to get to spend that special time with you, Hazel. Thanks to all of you!

Thank you to Joe Perry, my agent, for continuing to support me and my work. You are amazing!

Preface

I first attended a Disney Parks ticketed seasonal party in 2021, when my son Elliot and I dressed up as Lightning McQueen and a pit crew member to enjoy Oogie Boogie Bash at Disney California Adventure. Even though Elliot didn't last until the end of the party (he was only eight), I was hooked on the experience. The thinner crowds, the exclusive character meet and greets, the pumping music, and the *food*! There was so much food exclusive to the event that was expertly themed and absolutely delicious. That is when I decided to write a Disney Holidays cookbook, so everyone could have that exclusive, one-of-a-kind party experience—any day they want.

Since then, I have visited as many parties at Disney Parks as possible—but I've noticed that it isn't just the ticketed parties that have fun seasonal food items. Disney Parks take any excuse they can to introduce a new snack or treat, and holidays are the perfect opportunity. Throughout the last two years, I have been actively seeking out these food items and tasting them to see which ones are worthy of being offered in this cookbook. And I believe that I have found the most yummy, most fun, most photographable foods from Disney Parks' seasonal menus. I'm proud to share them here.

I believe that holidays are made to bring people together, and what brings people together best is good food. So keep this book handy on your counter all year round, because there is something for every month of the year!

Introduction

Disney Parks have incredible food offered every day at their theme parks across the world. While many are offered regularly (like the classic Dole Whip and Mickey pretzels), there are also special treats that you can only find during the most wonderful times of year: the holidays! From Easter and the Fourth of July to Hanukkah and New Year's Eve, there is something to celebrate at Disney Parks every season—and unique bites and sips to enjoy during each holiday.

The Unofficial Disney Parks Holidays Cookbook contains one hundred of the most iconic seasonal offerings from all six US Disney Parks, as well as the Resort Hotels and Entertainment Districts. With restaurants, food carts, and more spread across Disneyland, Magic Kingdom, EPCOT, Disney's Hollywood Studios, Disney's Animal Kingdom, Disney California Adventure, Disney Springs, Downtown Disney District, and Disney Resort Hotels, there are scrumptiously festive options everywhere you turn. Organized by Park location, the chapters that follow feature recipes that bring the magic of Disney and its holiday festivities to your own home. Although you might see some of these treats every year, a number of them are one-time creations made specially for different celebrations! You'll:

- Get into the Christmas spirit with Mickey Gingerbread and Frozen Salted Caramel Hot Chocolate.

- Celebrate Black History Month with Baked Andouille Mac & Cheese and Berry Beignets.

- Share Valentine's Day goodies like Strawberry Red Velvet Whoopie Pies and the Love Potion with your special one.

- Ring in the Lunar New Year with Surf & Turf Fried Rice and Green Tea Horchata.

- Show your pride during Pride Month with Rainbow Layer Cake and Celebration Sundaes.

- Get spooky for Halloween with Trick or Treat Sweets Churros and Blood Orange Slush.

- And more!

There are simple and easy dishes to whip up when you want a bit of holiday cheer any time of the year, as well as more-involved recipes to impress family and friends as you enjoy your favorite annual traditions together.

But before you become the Santa Claus or Easter Bunny in your own kitchen, read through Part 1 to learn more about the Disney seasonal offerings featured in Part 2, as well as what kitchen tools and pantry staples you'll want to have on hand. With these basics, you'll be ready to celebrate that next occasion in a delicious way.

So turn the page, and let's infuse the joy of the holidays with some Disney magic!

Disney Parks Holidays

Although park-goers have come to know, love, and expect certain food and drink items at Disney Parks when they visit, it is always fun to find new food and beverage offerings, especially limited-time seasonal ones!

In this part, you'll find everything you need to make the festive recipes found in Part 2. In Chapter 1, you will dive deeper into how Disney celebrates the holidays throughout the year and what delicious offerings you may find during each celebration. Then, in Chapter 2, you will take a peek at the equipment you will want to have on hand to create the recipes in this book. With the information in these chapters, you'll be ready to make your kitchen into a Disney holiday wonderland! And if you ever need a refresher while cooking, simply flip back to these pages.

CHAPTER 1

Celebrating All Year Long at the Disney Parks

Disney Parks have never been known to hold back on any celebrations, and holidays are no exception. Along with new characters, shows, decorations, music, and merchandise, one of the best parts of any Disney holiday celebration is discovering what new and exciting seasonal foods and drinks will be served.

In this chapter, you'll take a closer look at some of the most popular holidays celebrated at Disney Parks, as well as ones you maybe haven't heard of before. You'll learn about Disney ticketed parties and festivals, as well as the best places to look for seasonal treats while on vacation. Lastly, you'll discover how you can apply the recipes in this book to your own holiday menus throughout the year. So, before you pull on the oven mitts and turn up the festive music, take a look through the chapter ahead!

HOW DISNEY DOES HOLIDAYS

When Walt Disney dreamed up Disneyland on a park bench in California, he wanted a place where kids and adults alike could gather for a day of fun and family-friendly entertainment. Coming from the midwestern United States, Walt adored the small town feel of a Main Street lined with shops, and horses with carriages trundling down the drag. But he also wanted Disneyland to feel like a celebration, with marching bands, parades, and fireworks each and every day. People flocked to Disneyland to discover what that felt like, to make any day of the week a holiday. And if a normal day feels like a celebration, you can imagine how big actual holiday celebrations are at Disney Parks! Guests can experience not only fireworks and parades but also holiday-specific decorations and, of course, food! Incredible seasonal offerings dot the Parks to truly accentuate those special days of the year.

Lunar New Year

The first holiday of the year celebrated at Disney is the Lunar New Year, which observes the first new moon of the year, an important event for many cultures, particularly in Asia. Every year in late January to mid-February, Disney California Adventure holds a Lunar New Year celebration. Southern California has a strong connection to Asia, as many people from countries of the East immigrated to California through Angel Island and have maintained an important community in California ever since.

During the Lunar New Year celebration, guests can expect food booths brimming with special treats, entertainment just for the event, and fun merchandise available for purchase. The Park also offers a Sip and Savor Pass, which includes six coupons the holder can redeem for select offerings at participating booths. Among the most popular food items are the Pork and Shrimp Wontons with a Black Garlic Sauce served at Wrapped with Love and the Mickey Mouse–Shaped Hot Dog Buns from Bamboo Blessings (both temporary instillation booths at the Park). In addition to the food offerings, look around for festive decorations throughout the Park as well, including lanterns, red envelopes, character costumes, and a grand welcome archway.

Valentine's Day

Who wouldn't want to spend the most romantic day of the year with their love at a Disney Park? That's why Disney started offering a special after-hours ticketed event on several dates throughout January and February called "Sweethearts Nite." These nights come with exclusive photo opportunities throughout Disneyland with famous Disney couples like Cinderella and Prince Charming, Tiana and Naveen, Belle and The Beast, and more. And of course, what would a date be without food? Specialty sweets and drinks pop up just for the evening. It is a night to remember!

The rest of the Disney Parks, Resort Hotels, and Entertainment Districts also turn their hearts to Valentine's Day, with romance-themed foods across the board. Strawberry Red Velvet Whoopie Pies at The Trolley Car Café at Disney's Hollywood Studios and Strawberry S'mores at The Ganachery in Disney Springs are great examples of the eye-popping themed desserts available during this holiday. Also peep incredible floral designs and decor that will have everyone feeling warm, loving feelings during February.

Black History Month/Celebrate Soulfully

In the United States of America, February is Black History Month, which is marked with celebrations and acknowledgment of the Black community for their past, present, and future contributions to the country. Disney Parks created their own holiday to mirror Black History Month called "Celebrate Soulfully." You can see signs of Celebrate Soulfully across the Parks, Resort Hotels, and Entertainment Districts, with musical performances, art exhibits, merchandise, and an abundance of soul food.

Soul food is a type of cuisine traditionally made by Black people in the southern United States. Berry Beignets, Baked Andouille Mac & Cheese, and Sweet Potato Lunch Box Tarts are just a sampling of the foods you might find during the celebration in February. Be sure to look for postings at each food establishment for available Celebrate Soulfully dishes or beverages.

St. Patrick's Day

While most of the Disney Parks don't do much for St. Patrick's Day, there is one big exception: Raglan Road at Disney Springs. This eatery is an authentic Irish pub and has live music and dancing nightly. Guests can witness hard shoe dancing right near their table while eating corned beef and cabbage and drinking a Guinness. While every night is Irish at Raglan Road, on March 17, they deck the place out in shamrocks and green banners to add to the excitement. Be sure to make a reservation well in advance if you want to eat at Raglan Road on St. Patrick's Day, as they tend to fill up!

Additionally, Disneyland plays a fun leprechaun trick on the Grey Stuff at the Red Rose Taverne to make it the Green Stuff seasonally for St. Patrick's Day, and Beaches & Cream Soda Shop at Disney's Beach Club Resort serves up Mickey Shamrock Milk Shakes. Take a look around several Quick Service locations with seasonal mini treats available.

Easter

Easter is a holiday with Christian roots that now includes customs with many participants regardless of religious background. One of the most fun parts of Easter is an Easter egg hunt, and Disney wanted in on the action. Disneyland hosts a hunt called "Eggtravaganza," where kids of all ages can search high and low throughout the Park for eggs resembling Disney characters. If you locate them all, you win a prize! As a natural match due to its springtime run-dates, the EPCOT International Flower & Garden Festival incorporates a hunt for colorful eggs.

Many Easter goodies can be found at Disney Resort Hotels, where guests can wake up on Easter morning and treat themselves to something sweet, like the Peanut Butter Eggs from Contempo Café or the Thumper Carrot Cake available across several properties. Easter treats feature fun spring colors and egg or bunny motifs, as do the decorations scattered around the Parks.

May the Fourth

If you aren't a Star Wars fan, you might not have heard of this holiday before. As a play on words of the famous Star Wars line "May the Force be with you," May the Fourth became a fan holiday for Star Wars diehards to watch the movies and celebrate together. Disney didn't want to miss out on the fun, especially after their acquisition of Lucasfilm and the Star Wars franchise in 2012. Every year, Disney introduces more and more May the Fourth merchandise and food options as Star Wars continues to grow in popularity with new shows and movies continuously releasing in theaters and on Disney+. Treats like the Chocolate Chip Sweet-Sand Cookie sold at the Milk Stand at Disneyland and the Interstellar Sweet and Crunchy Popcorn at Disney's Hollywood Studios sell out fast to hungry fans.

In order to celebrate Star Wars for more than just one day, Disneyland dubbed April and May the "Season of the Force" beginning in 2024. During this time of the year only, a special nighttime fireworks vantage point can be enjoyed from Star Wars: Galaxy's Edge in Disneyland, including music by John Williams. An out-of-this-world overlay dons Hyperspace Mountain, turning the classic Space Mountain into a Star Wars adventure. Magic Shots by Disney PhotoPass Service lets guests hold a "holopuck" and seemingly receive communications from Din Djarin or Grogu! And best of all, yummy exclusive treats make a debut or a welcome return in the Park, like the Wookiee Cookie at Disney's Grand Californian Hotel & Spa.

Pride Month

Pride Month is celebrated globally in June to recognize the LGBTQIA+ community. Disney Parks have historically been a haven for people of diverse backgrounds, including LGBTQIA+ people, and they want to give back to this community by making the Parks a Pride playground during June. In 1991, guests at Walt Disney World in Florida unofficially began celebrating Gay Days by rallying the LGBTQIA+ community and their allies to wear red and show pride at Disney Parks on a certain day of each year. Members and allies in California caught on and began holding their own annual event at Disneyland in 1998. Disney Parks loved the idea and has expanded their offerings for Pride Month in June every year since. This includes colorful rainbow merchandise and food offerings throughout the month to let LGBTQIA+ members and allies know they are loved and wanted at Disney.

Some delightful food options include the Pride Artisan Marshmallows from Gasparilla's Island Grill and the stunning Rainbow Layer Cake from Sprinkles. Among the decorations that spring up during Pride Month are several photo backgrounds featuring the classic rainbow design, as well as the word "LOVE" to take a photograph in front of and share your own love with the world.

Fourth of July

Disney knows that they have an international palette of guests visiting the Parks, but Walt Disney was a staunch American patriot and wanted his theme Parks to represent that too. The first ever animatronic at Disneyland was of Abraham Lincoln because Walt admired him so much. Certain spots in the Parks are also homages to America, like Liberty Square in Magic Kingdom and The American Adventure pavilion at EPCOT. Liberty Square's Columbia Harbour House makes a special Berry Shortcake for the Fourth of July that shouldn't be missed. Disney prepares for this holiday as one of the busiest days of the year at the Parks with tons of food and fun. In addition to treats like the Lunch Box Parfait at Disney's Hollywood Studios and the Experiment 0341: Red, White, and Blue Slush from Disney California Adventure, Magic Kingdom puts on an impressive fireworks display costing upward of $10,000 per show! American flags and banners can also be seen adorning lampposts and doorways all down Main Street U.S.A. to celebrate the occasion.

Halloween

For Disney Parks, Halloween rivals Christmas as the biggest holiday of the year. Due to its popularity, Mickey's Not-So-Scary Halloween Party at Magic Kingdom now starts in August, and tickets for Oogie Boogie Bash at Disney California Adventure routinely sell out in minutes each year. In 2023, servers crashed moments into the sale of Oogie Boogie Bash tickets from the thousands of fans trying to snag them!

Mickey's Not-So-Scary Halloween Party at Magic Kingdom features the Mickey's Boo-To-You Halloween Parade down Main Street U.S.A., led by the Headless Horseman himself, and includes ballroom-dancing ghosts, gravediggers, pirates, and more. The *Hocus Pocus* Villain Spelltacular is a show in front of Cinderella Castle starring the Sanderson Sisters along with dozens of other spooky characters strutting their stuff onstage. The Cadaver Dans barbershop quartet croons over in Frontierland, while dance parties are hosted across the Park. Spots where you can trick-or-treat are signaled by large balloons and can be visited as many times as you like! Guests are often seen dressed in elaborate costumes for Mickey's Not-So-Scary Halloween Party, and Disney characters are dressed in Halloween costumes as well.

In addition, exclusive food and drinks are available around the Park, such as The Doom Berry drink from Sleepy Hollow, the Un Poco Loco Tots from The Friar's Nook, and the Spellbinding Fried Pie from Golden Oak Outpost. Almost every eatery has at least one or two exclusive items just for the party, and guests line up to get their hands on them. The Almond Sweet Corn Cake from Pecos Bill Tall Tale Inn and Cafe sells out each night, usually within an hour.

Most of the fanfare of Halloween is centralized to Magic Kingdom and Disney California Adventure (where the ticketed parties are), but other Parks, Resorts, and Entertainment Districts also like to get in on the fun with spooky (or not-so-spooky) Halloween decorations and seasonal treats, like the Candy Corn Milkshake from Disney's Hollywood Studios or the Blood Orange Slush from Disneyland.

Thanksgiving

Thanksgiving isn't a very big "commercial" holiday in the United States, but what it is big on is *food*. Many children have school off for the end of Thanksgiving week, which certainly upticks the attendance at Disney Parks, and Disney wanted to provide the traditional Thanksgiving fixings across the Parks and Resort Hotels for their guests. Much of the Thanksgiving offerings feature flavors that people know and love, like the Thanksgiving Leftover Sandwich from Chef Art Smith's Homecomin' (full of turkey, stuffing, and cranberry) or the Pumpkin Tart at Disney Resort Hotels. Disney understands what people are looking for on Thanksgiving and provides it! Parks' decor includes autumnal theming such as leaves and cornucopias.

Christmas

For many, Christmas is truly the most wonderful time of the year. Across America, shops are brimming with flashy decor, and people hang lights on their homes and put up a Christmas tree inside, among countless other traditions. Because Christmas began as a religious holiday, the birth of Jesus Christ is often celebrated. And of course, there's the food! Traditional meals of turkey, ham, mashed potatoes, cranberry sauce, stuffing, and more are often served. Desserts like pumpkin pie, fruitcake, sugar cookies, and candies are eaten in abundance.

So, since Disney Parks are set up to be like a holiday every day, how do they make a major holiday like Christmas stand out? How do they honor the traditions that people hold so dear while offering something new and exciting to entice visitors?

From the Parks' inception, Christmastime has been met with festive decor and tasty holiday treats. But in 1983, Walt Disney World held the first ever Mickey's Very Merry Christmas Party. This was an after-hours extra-ticket event mirroring the super-popular Grad Nite events that had been going on at Disneyland since 1961. During Grad Nite, daytime guests of the Park would leave by a certain time, and guests with a Grad Nite "party" ticket would get wristbands to allow them access to the events of the night. And since each party ticket usually costs around the same price as a whole day in the Park, Disney knew they needed to provide value to entice people to buy the tickets. Grad Nite tickets were limited to high school seniors and their chaperones, so a Christmas Party would be the first open-ticket purchase available.

At Walt Disney World, Mickey's Very Merry Christmas Party usually begins with guests receiving a special little gift (like an ornament) to commemorate the evening. Guests are then treated to several hours full of fun activities and exclusive bonuses only offered during the party. In 2023, these were the offerings: Mickey's Once Upon a Christmastime Parade thundered down Main Street U.S.A., featuring a tin soldier marching band, dancing reindeer, and the Big Man himself, Santa Claus; *Frozen*'s Queen Elsa used her powers to light Cinderella Castle; Mickey and Friends performed a special show called "Mickey's Most Merriest Celebration" on the castle stage, which included singing and dancing, and special character meet and greets popping up all around the Park, with most characters in holiday attire just for the party. Offerings vary from year to year but typically follow this layout.

Many special snacks, treats, and drinks are also offered throughout the Park during Mickey's Very Merry Christmas Party, like the Chai-Caramel Freeze at Golden Oak Outpost, the Christmas Wreath Doughnuts on Main Street U.S.A., and the Sugar Plum Shake from Auntie Gravity's Galactic Goodies.

Complimentary treats are offered throughout the Park during the party, with each stop including a hot beverage and a cookie. Trying to collect all of them is a game in and of itself! Not only are yummy sweets available for free; many snacks, treats, and drinks are reserved just for the party.

The party always ends with a "Holiday Wishes" fireworks show that lights up the sky over Cinderella Castle with holiday-themed music, lights, and projections. It is not uncommon to see guests dressed up in holiday costumes or matching group apparel, as the party has grown into a tradition that people enjoy year after year. Tickets usually sell out for most dates months in advance. People love all the exciting offerings, and especially that they are exclusive.

At Disneyland, ticketed Christmas parties have only been offered since 2021 and are called "Disney Merriest Nites." Since a large portion of Disneyland's guests are locals, the "exclusive" options and advance ticket sales aren't as popular as at Disney World, where most guests aren't local. So before 2021, holiday cheer was available to everyone at the Park. Even with the party happening on select nights, regular Disneyland guests can delight in decorations around Main Street U.S.A., a Christmas Fantasy Parade, a "Believe... In Holiday Magic" fireworks show, and various festive "overlays" on classic attractions like "it's a small world" and Haunted Mansion. (An "overlay" doesn't change the track of a ride but instead gives new decorations, music, and sometimes scents to the ride! Haunted Mansion Holiday famously adds the smell of gingerbread to the ballroom scene for a delicious change.) There are also plenty of holiday goodies for sale across the Park, like the Christmas Punch at Galactic Grill or the ultra-popular Mickey Gingerbread at Jolly Holiday Bakery Cafe.

But Disneyland isn't the only Park that has holiday fun for all. EPCOT International Festival of the Holidays and Disney Festival of Holidays at Disney California Adventure are also open to anyone with a Park ticket. EPCOT booths mostly highlight festive foods from around the world, like Las Posadas Holiday Kitchen in the Mexico pavilion, Prost! in the Germany pavilion, and Shanghai Holiday Kitchen in the China pavilion.

Disney California Adventure takes traditional holiday bites and gives them an elevated twist, like at the Heritage Cottage and Merry Mashups booths. Each festival also includes entertainment and offerings that are only available during festival time, such as listening to the Canadian Holiday Voyageurs sing acapella Christmas tunes or meeting Père Noël (a French version of Santa Claus) in the France pavilion. Exclusive merchandise abounds, such as holiday-themed Spirit Jerseys and home decor. The other US Disney Parks also pull out the trappings during this time and decorate with holly, lights, wreaths, and more to brighten the holiday season.

EPCOT and Disneyland hold several Candlelight Processionals during this time each year, in which celebrity hosts, with a choir and orchestra, tell the story of the birth of Jesus. As part of their holiday celebrations, many people enjoy the Christmas tradition of a procession, and Disney Parks wanted to provide that experience for their guests. The first Candlelight Processional at Disneyland was held in 1958, only three years after the Park opened, making it a long-running tradition that continues to this day.

Hanukkah

Disney Parks honor and celebrate Hanukkah, an important event within the Jewish faith. At EPCOT, you can find the L'Chaim! Holiday Kitchen celebrating Hanukkah with Jewish-inspired dishes such as Black and White Cookies and Smoked Salmon Potato Latkes. Between the Morocco and France pavilions, look out for the Hanukkah Storyteller, who regales audiences with the story of the Macabees with delightful enthusiasm and beautiful fiddle accompaniment. And while there are not a lot of Hanukkah decorations in the Parks, more and more merchandise offerings are becoming available, such as kitchen items and menorahs to take home.

New Year's Eve

The last holiday of the year celebrated at Disney is New Year's Eve. Some Disney Parks keep their doors open past midnight to allow guests to ring in the New Year while riding an attraction. EPCOT even stations DJs around the Park to host a massive dance party and projects the countdown onto Spaceship Earth. But many people choose to bring the party back to their Resort Hotel and clink a couple Champagne Beignets together while counting down. The Parks and Resorts of Disney have great options available for both the late-night party animal and the not-so-much.

BRINGING DISNEY HOLIDAYS HOME

When you are celebrating a holiday at home, you can celebrate it however you want. You can make every recipe in this book during the corresponding holiday, decorate to the nines, and invite all your friends and family members over for the festivities. Or you can mix up one of the drinks or whip up one of the treats any day of the week and bring the holiday to you. However you love to celebrate, this book is here to assist you. Holidays exist to bring people together, to give you something to look forward to, and to enable you to show love and care for those around you. So look ahead to your upcoming week, month, or year, and bring these recipes along for your own Disney-inspired celebrations!

CHAPTER 2

The Disney Parks Cook's Essentials

Holidays at the Disney Parks are so exciting—and you can make your home kitchen just as fun. In the chapter ahead, you will explore the equipment and ingredients needed to create the recipes in Part 2. Don't feel like you need to sit down and read the details of every item before turning to the recipes: This chapter can be used as a guide for when you have a question about a particular tool or ingredient mentioned in a recipe you want to make.

Some of the best resources here are substitution suggestions. If you don't have a certain piece of equipment, don't fret; more likely than not, there is an easy swap available that you may already have! So flip through this chapter and take note of any equipment and ingredients you might need later, then start whipping up holiday magic at home!

EQUIPMENT AND FOOD STAPLES

The festivities await you, but are you ready to get cooking? Before you start, take a look through the following sections to make sure your kitchen is stocked with all the tools needed to make the recipes in Part 2.

Air Fryer

An air fryer reaches high temperatures and circulates heat quickly within a compact space to crisp up foods, giving them a "fried" taste. If you don't have an air fryer, simply use your standard oven and cook as instructed. You may need to add more time, so keep an eye on the food as it cooks.

Baking Sheets

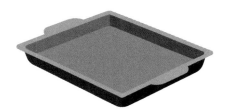

Baking sheets come in many shapes and sizes. The most common sheets have a ½" rim around all the edges and come in three sizes: quarter sheets, half sheets, and full sheets. Quarter sheets are 9" × 13", half sheets are 13" × 18", and full sheets are 26" × 18". Most of the recipes that follow use the half-sheet variety, though any of the sizes work equally well.

Blender

A good-quality, high-powered stand blender helps achieve a smoother consistency in recipes like smoothies and dips. Start with a low setting and turn up the speed as ingredients start to break up.

Cake Pans

Standard 9" circle and square metal cake pans will help you create cakes and other tasty treats. Typically, you will want to line these pans with parchment paper to prevent sticking.

Cocktail Shaker

A cocktail shaker makes mixing easy for single-serve mixed drinks. You can also quickly chill a drink during mixing by adding ice to the shaker before shaking. Most standard shakers hold 24 ounces of liquid. If you don't have a cocktail shaker, you can whisk the mixture in a large glass cup or small bowl and strain through a sieve.

Coffee Substitute

Some people don't like coffee or might want to enjoy a coffee-style drink without caffeine later in the day. Many coffee-substitute, caffeine-free products are available at stores and online retailers. Most are made from malted barley, chicory, and rye. Pero and Caf-Lib are great choices, as they don't require the use of a coffee machine. Just follow the instructions on the packaging, then add to the recipe in place of coffee or cold brew.

Cooling Rack

A common wire cooling/drying rack is sufficient for the recipes in this book. Cooling racks are typically made from stainless steel and have straight lines or a crosshatch pattern.

Food Coloring

A number of recipes in this book use food coloring to create the original look found in the parks. Gel colors are best for solid foods, while liquid colors are best for drinks. Gel colors have a brighter pop of color than liquid food coloring, and the dense consistency won't change the texture of the food. If your gel colors come in pots and cannot "drop," use a wooden toothpick to dip into the gel and swipe it through the food you want to color. Repeat for each drop needed.

Food Processor

Food processors specialize in chopping dry foods. If you don't have a food processor, a high-powered blender will work. If you have neither, you can chop the ingredients very finely with a knife—the pieces may just be less uniform.

Frosting

Many grocery stores carry ready-made tubs or bags of frosting, available in all colors. Having these on hand is perfect for adding little details on top of desserts without having to make another batch of frosting from scratch. If you would rather make homemade frosting for recipes, here is a simple formula: 1 cup softened butter, 2 cups powdered sugar, 2 tablespoons whipping cream, and food coloring. This yields about the same as a typical tub of frosting from the store. Adjust the confectioners' sugar and whipping cream to meet the desired texture in the recipe.

Glass Pan

A number of recipes in this book use 8" × 8" glass pans. A metal pan can be substituted if you don't have glass; just be sure to check the food more often to prevent overcooking.

Grill or Grill Pan

For ingredients that need to be grilled, an outdoor grill and indoor grill pan are interchangeable for searing food items. Propane grills should be preheated to ensure even cooking. Indoor grill pans need to be greased with cooking oil before use to help prevent sticking. Charcoal grills can also be used. Look to your grill instructions for safe cooking guidelines.

Ice Cream Machine

The easiest ice cream machines are the ones with a freezable "bowl." This bowl is removed from the freezer right before use, and cream or drink mix is poured directly into the frozen bowl. The bowl then spins on a base, and a paddle mixes and scrapes the inside. Other options are also available, such as an ice cream bucket–type machine. Pour the mixture from the recipe into the metal inner container and fill the outer bucket with  ice and rock salt. Run the machine until the consistency matches the recipe description. Another common type is the Ninja CREAMi. Simply freeze the recipe mixture in the provided containers for 24 hours, then run in the machine using the "ice cream" or "sorbet" setting. Any machine you have on hand is fine.

Jellyroll Pan

Jellyroll pans have slightly different dimensions than other sheet pans. They are usually 15" × 10" but otherwise look like a sheet pan. This more elongated shape allows  more rolls in a jellyroll dish. This pan is used for Maple Bûche de Noël in this book. You can get a jellyroll pan from online retailers, or if you don't want to buy one, substitute in a quarter baking pan and don't pour all the batter into the pan. Just add batter to just below the lip of the pan and discard the remaining batter.

Molds

Some recipes in this book require the use of molds. Silicone or plastic molds work well; just make sure plastic ones are rated to withstand the temperatures of hot candy and won't melt when poured into.

Parchment Paper

Almost every recipe in this book that involves baking will instruct you to line the baking sheet or pan with parchment paper. This ensures a more even baking surface and more consistent browning, and it greatly reduces the chances of the food sticking to the pan. Parchment paper can be found in any grocery store or online.

Pie Weights

Pie weights are beads that are used to fill a pie crust that is being "blind-baked," or baked without filling. The weight simulates filling so the crust cooks more evenly and holds its shape. If you don't have pie weights, uncooked dried beans or rice work just as well.

Piping Bags

Many recipes in this book use piping bags, but a heavy-duty plastic sandwich or gallon bag will do nicely if you don't have any on hand. Just scoop the mixture into the bag, then snip a small edge off one of the bottom corners. Start the hole out small and make it bigger as needed.

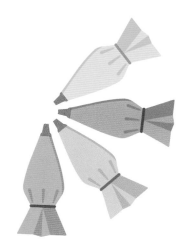

Piping Bag Tips

Some recipes in this book call for special piping bag tips. While you don't *need* to use a tip for any recipe in this book, it can make for an impressive design.

Pots and Pans

Heavy-bottomed saucepans are preferred over other types for the recipes in this book. The thick metal bottom regulates the temperature better and prevents burning. If you don't have heavy-bottomed pans, any appropriately sized pot or pan will do; just keep an extra-close eye on foods cooking on the stove. Stir more frequently to prevent burning. Nonstick pans are not usually necessary but are helpful in some recipes, The nonstick surface allows the batter to slide off without sticking. If you don't have a nonstick pan, grease the pan with plenty of nonstick cooking spray or oil before cooking.

Rolling Pin

Rolling pins come in many shapes and sizes, including those that have handles on the sides, French styles, and straight cylinder styles. Any rolling pin you have on hand can be used in the following recipes.

Sieve/Sifter

The sieves/sifters used in the following recipes refer to a stainless-steel mesh half-dome strainer. Get one with a medium-fine mesh for best results.

Stand Mixer

Almost every recipe in this book that calls for mixing uses a stand mixer. This machine makes mixing, whipping, and kneading easy and uniform. If you don't have a stand mixer, you can use a hand mixer, which often also has interchangeable attachments for mixing or whipping. If you have neither, you can mix, whip, or knead by hand.

Syrups

Syrups are a crucial part of making many mixed drinks in the Parks. They typically use the brand Monin for drinks instead of house-made syrups. This provides consistency and high quality across the Parks and is especially useful when drinks change locations—which they often do. If you can't find Monin syrups, other brands work just as well.

Tart Pan

The recipes for Pumpkin Tart and St. Patrick's Day Irish Coffee Tarts call for a 4" tart pan (or two). This pan has a removable circular bottom and a flat ring that makes up the side of the pan. You can use this kind of pan, or you can use the more common scalloped version. If you have neither, use the bottom of a jumbo muffin tin and press the dough into the bottom and along the bottom side 1" to make the tart crust.

Thermometer

A confection or candy thermometer is essential for candy making and deep-frying. Bringing mixtures to the correct temperature will ensure the desired texture and taste. A meat thermometer should be used to ensure meat is cooked to a safe temperature. Both types of thermometers can be bought at most grocery and big-box stores or online.

GETTING THE FESTIVITIES STARTED

Now you've got the knowledge, and you've got the tools, so what are you waiting for? It's time to dive into deliciously fun recipes that will make every day of the year full of holiday fun. Remember to take your time and make each recipe yours as you see fit; it is your kitchen and they are your creations, so enjoy the experience!

PART 2

Disney Parks Holidays Recipes

It's time to get cooking! Ahead are one hundred recipes for an array of holidays throughout the year. Even if there is a recipe from a holiday you don't typically celebrate, give it a try! It may become a new mainstay in your household. Also remember that these recipes are yours to play with. Disney Parks serve their food in a standardized way, but you have the ability to customize any recipe as you like. In fact, one of the most fun ways to tailor a recipe is to change the holiday! A simple frosting color or sprinkle shape swap can take a Halloween treat and make it ready for the Fourth of July.

The chapters in this part are organized by Park: Disneyland; Magic Kingdom; EPCOT; Disney's Hollywood Studios & Disney's Animal Kingdom; Disney California Adventure; Disney Springs & Downtown Disney District; and finally, Disney Resort Hotels. If you are searching for a specific holiday to celebrate, simply flip to the back of the book where you'll find a special index of recipes organized by holiday. Now, let the celebrating begin!

CHAPTER 3

Disneyland

Welcome to Disneyland, where the spirit of holiday fun has been enchanting families since 1955! Walt Disney's vision of a place where everyone could experience the joy of celebration comes alive in this chapter, bursting with recipes for your own culinary adventures throughout the holidays.

Prepare to be swept away by festive treats for Valentine's Day, Black History Month/Celebrate Soulfully, St. Patrick's Day, May the Fourth, Halloween, and Christmas! Imagine whipping up those irresistible Chocolate Chip Sweet-Sand Cookies from Galaxy's Edge for a Star Wars marathon with friends. Or honoring Black History Month by cooking up a filling meal of Shrimp & Grits from Cafe Orleans. And don't forget to quench your thirst! Sip on the sweet nostalgia of Christmas Punch from Galactic Grill or warm up during the chilly season with Peppermint Hot Chocolate from French Market Restaurant. Every recipe in this chapter is an invitation to bring the magic of the holidays at Disneyland home, transforming your kitchen into a wonderland of deliciousness. No lines to wait in here—just pure happiness to savor.

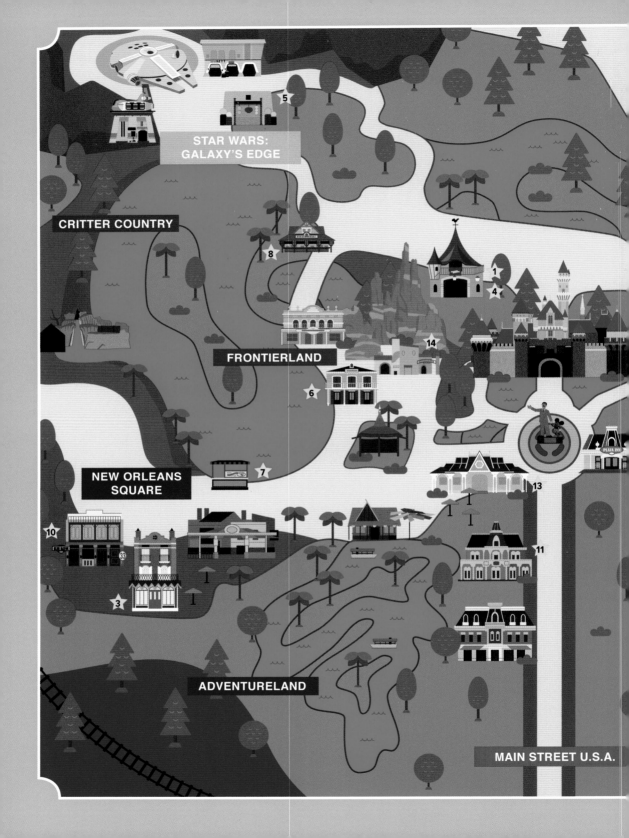

STAR WARS: GALAXY'S EDGE

5

CRITTER COUNTRY

8

FRONTIERLAND

1
4

14

6

NEW ORLEANS SQUARE

7

10

33

13

11

3

ADVENTURELAND

PLAZA INN

MAIN STREET U.S.A.

DISNEYLAND

1. **HEART-SHAPED BUTTER COOKIES**
   (Red Rose Taverne, Valentine's Day)

2. **GALACTIC SUNRISE SLUSH**
   (Galactic Grill, Valentine's Day)

3. **SHRIMP & GRITS**
   (Cafe Orleans, Black History Month/Celebrate Soulfully)

4. **GREEN STUFF**
   (Red Rose Taverne, St. Patrick's Day)

5. **CHOCOLATE CHIP SWEET-SAND COOKIES**
   (Milk Stand, May the Fourth)

6. **PURPLE SABER FUNNEL CAKES**
   (Stage Door Café, May the Fourth)

7. **TRICK OR TREAT SWEETS CHURROS**
   (Churros Cart, New Orleans Square, Halloween)

8. **PUMPKIN CHURRO FUNNEL CAKE**
   (Hungry Bear Restaurant, Halloween)

9. **BLOOD ORANGE SLUSH**
   (Galactic Grill, Halloween)

10. **PEPPERMINT HOT CHOCOLATE**
    (French Market Restaurant, Christmas)

11. **PEPPERMINT HOLIDAY SUNDAES**
    (Gibson Girl Ice Cream Parlor, Christmas)

12. **CHRISTMAS PUNCH**
    (Galactic Grill, Christmas)

13. **MICKEY GINGERBREAD**
    (Jolly Holiday Bakery Cafe, Christmas)

14. **CALDO DE POLLO**
    (Rancho del Zocalo Restaurante, Christmas)

Heart-Shaped Butter Cookies

Red Rose Taverne, Valentine's Day

· · · ✦ · · ·

Picture this: gifting a vibrantly colored box adorned with crimson roses and bursting with Heart-Shaped Butter Cookies. It's the perfect treat for someone special—be that a friend or a sweetheart. If you're enjoying these goodies from Red Rose Taverne in Disneyland, share a cookie and climb aboard the nearby King Arthur Carousel, letting the merry-go-round carry you away on a whirlwind of laughter and love. Hold hands, savor the treat, and spin into a fairy tale where every bite is happily ever after.

MAKES 12 COOKIES

1 cup salted butter, softened

1 cup granulated sugar

2 large eggs

2 teaspoons vanilla extract

1/4 teaspoon almond extract

1/2 teaspoon salt

1 teaspoon baking powder

2 1/2 cups all-purpose flour

1. In bowl of a stand mixer fitted with paddle attachment, cream together butter and sugar on medium speed until well combined and fluffy, about 2 minutes. Add in eggs, vanilla and almond extracts, salt, and baking powder and mix 1 minute more. Reduce speed to low and slowly add in flour while mixer continues to run on low speed until all flour is added and mixture is uniform.

2. Cut dough in half and flatten each half into a 1/2"-thick disk and wrap in plastic wrap. Refrigerate 30 minutes.

3. Preheat oven to 350°F and line two full-sized baking sheets with parchment paper. Set aside.

(continued) ▶

12 tablespoons premade white cookie icing

12 teaspoons Valentine's sprinkles (red and pink mini hearts and white mini balls)

12 candy bows, red with white dots

12 tablespoons seedless raspberry jam

4. Working with one dough disk, sandwich dough between two sheets of parchment paper and roll out dough to $1/4$" thickness. Use a large (about 4" in diameter) heart-shaped cookie cutter to cut out 12 cookies. Place onto one prepared baking sheet and bake in preheated oven 10–12 minutes until bottoms are slightly browned. Remove from oven and allow to cool on pan 30 minutes.

5. Sandwich remaining dough between two sheets of parchment paper and roll out dough to $1/4$" thickness. Use a large (about 4" in diameter) heart-shaped cookie cutter to cut out 12 cookies, then use a smaller heart-shaped cookie cutter (about 3" in diameter) to remove centers of cookies. Discard excess dough. Place cookies on second prepared baking sheet and bake in preheated oven 10–12 minutes until bottoms are slightly browned. Remove from oven and allow to cool on pan 30 minutes.

6. Once all cookies are completely cooled, decorate cookies with cut-out centers by drizzling with white icing, topping with sprinkles, and placing a candy bow on each (adhered with a small dollop of icing). Allow icing to dry and harden, about 20 minutes.

7. Flip over each remaining cookie so that the flat bottoms are facing up. Spread a thin layer of jam across each cookie, leaving about $1/4$" border around sides. Carefully place decorated "border" cookies on top of jam. Allow to set about 10 minutes and enjoy.

Galactic Sunrise Slush

Galactic Grill, Valentine's Day

. . . ✦ . . .

If you're looking for something quick and easy to wow your sweetheart on Valentine's Day, here it is. The sweetness of fresh strawberries combines with the tartness of lime to please any palate. Galactic Grill often serves seasonal drinks and slushes, so always check the menu when you're in Tomorrowland to see what is being served up that day. Holidays can be celebrated in space too!

SERVES 2

- 8 large fresh strawberries, hulled and stems removed
- ¼ cup lime juice
- 1 cup cold water
- ¼ cup granulated sugar
- ¾ cup frozen strawberries
- 2 cups crushed ice
- ¼ cup strawberry syrup

1. Place 4 fresh strawberries each in the bottom of two 16-ounce plastic cups. Smush and muddle until a jam-like consistency forms. Set aside.

2. In the pitcher of a blender, add lime juice, water, sugar, frozen strawberries, ice, and strawberry syrup. Blend until smooth and pour evenly onto muddled strawberries in plastic cups. Insert large-gauge straws and serve immediately.

Disney Parks Tip

The Galactic Grill is a great place to stake out a "home base" in Tomorrowland, as Finding Nemo Submarine Voyage, Autopia, Buzz Lightyear Astro Blasters, and Space Mountain all circle the area.

Shrimp & Grits

Cafe Orleans, Black History Month/Celebrate Soulfully

. . . ✳ . . .

First made by America's indigenous people, grits were picked up by Black enslaved people in the American South. They harvested corn, ground it into a coarse meal, and then cooked it into a thick, creamy porridge, which was often served with a variety of toppings, such as shrimp, bacon, and eggs. Over time, grits became a popular dish throughout the South. When you eat shrimp and grits, you are not just enjoying a delicious meal; you are also celebrating the history and culture of African Americans. It is more than just food; it is a reminder of the strength and resilience of the enslaved people who created it.

SERVES 2

FOR CHEESY GRITS

2 cups water

1/2 cup 5-minute instant grits

1 1/2 cups sharp Cheddar cheese

2 tablespoons salted butter

2 tablespoons heavy whipping cream

1/2 teaspoon ground black pepper

FOR ANDOUILLE-FAVA RELISH

1 tablespoon olive oil

6 ounces diced cooked Andouille sausage

1/2 cup canned fava beans, drained and rinsed

1/4 cup diced white onion

1/4 cup diced Roma tomatoes

1. To make Cheesy Grits: Bring water to a boil in a small saucepan over medium heat. Add instant grits and stir until incorporated. Cook, stirring frequently, 5–7 minutes until all water is evaporated. Remove from heat and stir in cheese, butter, whipping cream, and black pepper. Set aside.

2. To make Andouille-Fava Relish: In a large skillet over medium heat, add oil and heat 2 minutes. Add sausage and heat 3 minutes or until sausage is browned. Add fava beans, onion, tomato, garlic, salt, and pepper and reduce heat to low. Simmer on low 15 minutes, stirring occasionally. Remove from heat and set aside.

3. To make Shrimp Sauce: In a small saucepan over medium heat, add whipping cream, paprika, chili powder, garlic powder, cayenne pepper, and chicken bouillon. Bring to a boil, then reduce heat to low and simmer 15 minutes, stirring occasionally. Remove from heat and set aside.

(continued) ▶

1 teaspoon minced garlic

1/2 teaspoon salt

1/2 teaspoon ground black pepper

FOR SHRIMP SAUCE

2 cups heavy whipping cream

1 teaspoon paprika

1 teaspoon chili powder

1 teaspoon garlic powder

1/8 teaspoon cayenne pepper

1 teaspoon chicken bouillon powder

FOR SHRIMP

2 tablespoons salted butter

12 extra-large raw shrimp, tails off

1 tablespoon paprika

1 tablespoon salt

FOR ASSEMBLY

4 stalks green onion, whites discarded, chopped diagonally into 1" pieces

4. To make Shrimp: In a medium skillet over medium heat, add butter and melt. Meanwhile, toss raw shrimp in paprika and salt until well coated. Cook seasoned shrimp in skillet 1–2 minutes per side until shrimp is no longer translucent and is cooked through. Set aside.

5. To Assemble: Scoop Cheesy Grits into two serving bowls. Drizzle desired amount of Shrimp Sauce on Grits. Scoop about 1/2 cup Andouille-Fava Relish on top of Grits (leftovers can be refrigerated in an airtight container up to 2 days) and top with 6 Shrimp each. Sprinkle green onion pieces on top and serve immediately.

Green Stuff

Red Rose Taverne, St. Patrick's Day

· · · ✦ · · ·

Disney fans know about the Grey Stuff (it's delicious!), but have you heard of the Green Stuff? This riff on the original usually served at the Red Rose Taverne invites you to enjoy a minty treat for the St. Patrick's Day holiday. Another fun variation is the Grave Stuff during Halloween time, which includes a cookie gravestone. However you like your "stuff" is up to you!

SERVES 12

FOR SHORTBREAD COOKIES

- **1 cup salted butter, softened**
- **½ cup plus 2 tablespoons granulated sugar, divided**
- **1 teaspoon vanilla extract**
- **2 cups all-purpose flour**

FOR CHOCOLATE CAKE

- **1 (15.25-ounce) box chocolate cake mix**
- **1¼ cups water**
- **½ cup vegetable oil**
- **3 large eggs**

1. Preheat oven to 350°F. Line an ungreased half-sized baking sheet with parchment paper and set aside.

2. To make Shortbread Cookies: In the bowl of a stand mixer, add butter and ½ cup sugar. Using paddle attachment, cream together well, then add vanilla and flour. Mix until dough is sticking together but still crumbly, about 2 minutes. Form into a ball by hand.

3. Sprinkle 1 tablespoon sugar across a flat surface and place dough ball on it. Sprinkle top of dough ball with remaining 1 tablespoon sugar and roll dough out to ¼" thickness.

4. Using a biscuit cutter (or a drinking glass flipped upside down), cut out 12 (3") circles in the dough.

5. Carefully transfer dough circles onto prepared baking sheet. Bake about 12 minutes or until circles look very light, with slight browning on the bottom. Allow to cool completely on the baking sheet, about 1 hour.

(continued) ▶

12 mint-flavored chocolate sandwich cookies

1 (3.4-ounce) box instant vanilla pudding

1½ cups whole milk

1 (8-ounce) tub frozen whipped topping, thawed

5 drops green gel food coloring

12 teaspoons mixed St. Patrick's Day sprinkles

6. To make Chocolate Cake: Preheat oven to 375°F.

7. In a large bowl, stir together cake mix, water, oil, and eggs about 1 minute. Scoop into a mini muffin tin, making at least 12 mini cakes (discard excess batter). Bake 12–14 minutes until a knife inserted comes out clean. Remove from oven and allow to cool completely in the pan, about 1 hour.

8. To make Green Stuff: In a blender or food processor, crush sandwich cookies into a fine crumble. Set aside.

9. In a large bowl, add instant pudding powder and milk. Whisk together and let chill in refrigerator 10 minutes. Once chilled, fold in cookie crumbles, whipped topping, and food coloring until just combined. Scoop into a large piping bag with a large star tip. Set aside.

10. To Assemble: Place one Shortbread Cookie on a serving plate. Squirt one dollop of Green Stuff onto Cookie and invert one Chocolate Cake onto cookie. In one smooth motion, swirl Green Stuff around Chocolate Cake from bottom to top in a conical shape. Finish with 1 teaspoon sprinkles. Repeat with remaining ingredients to make 12 servings. Serve immediately.

Chocolate Chip Sweet-Sand Cookies

Milk Stand, May the Fourth

. . . ✦ . . .

Resembling the famous ½-pound cookies sold at Gideon's Bakehouse in Disney Springs in Florida, this cookie made its debut at Galaxy's Edge in May 2022—and Californians couldn't get enough of it. While the cookie was only available for a short time, guests were buying them out early in the morning and causing long lines at the Milk Stand. It's no wonder, because these sweet and salty cookies are great any time—and any day of the year—and are super simple to prepare.

MAKES 10 EXTRA-LARGE COOKIES

1 cup salted butter, softened

1 cup light brown sugar

½ cup granulated sugar

1 tablespoon vanilla bean paste

2 large eggs

1 teaspoon baking powder

½ teaspoon baking soda

1 teaspoon salt

3 cups all-purpose flour

1½ cups large semisweet chocolate chips, divided

½ cup toffee bits

½ cup whole shelled pistachios

1. Preheat oven to 325°F. Line a full-sized baking sheet with parchment and set aside.

2. In bowl of a stand mixer fitted with paddle attachment, add butter and sugars. Mix 2 minutes or until well combined. Add in vanilla bean paste and eggs and mix 1 minute more. Add baking powder, baking soda, salt, and flour and stir 1 minute more or until well combined. Add in ½ cup chocolate chips and toffee bits and mix 1 additional minute.

3. Make 10 balls of dough using a large (3-tablespoon) cookie scoop and set on prepared baking sheet. Take each ball and press remaining 1 cup chocolate chips onto tops only (retaining ball shape). Press 5–6 pistachios into dough around chocolate chips. Return balls to sheet, evenly spaced out, and bake 15–18 minutes until edges begin to turn golden brown. Remove from oven and allow to cool on sheet 10 minutes. Eat warm or freeze for later. Frozen cookies last up to 1 month. Simply remove from freezer and thaw at room temperature before eating.

Purple Saber Funnel Cakes

Stage Door Café, May the Fourth

. . . ✦ . . .

There is a lot going on with this dessert, and with good reason: It combines equal parts red and blue, representing the balance between dark and light sides of the Force. Mace Windu wields the only purple lightsaber of the Jedi Council. While you won't see Mace Windu walking around Galaxy's Edge, some characters you might spot include Kylo Ren, Rey, Chewbacca, The Mandalorian (Din Djarin) and Grogu, Hera and Chopper, and Ahsoka!

SERVES 4

FOR MIXED BERRY SAUCE

- **3 cups frozen mixed berries**
- **1/4 cup plus 1 tablespoon water, divided**
- **2 tablespoons granulated sugar**
- **1 tablespoon cornstarch**

FOR CHOCOLATE FUNNEL CAKE

- **48 ounces vegetable oil, for frying**
- **1 large egg**
- **2/3 cup whole milk**
- **2 tablespoons granulated sugar**
- **1 1/4 cups all-purpose flour**
- **3 tablespoons cocoa powder**
- **1/4 teaspoon salt**
- **2 teaspoons baking powder**

1. For Mixed Berry Sauce: In a medium saucepan over medium heat, add berries, 1/4 cup water, and sugar. Stir frequently until mixture comes to a boil, then reduce heat to low. In a separate small bowl, combine cornstarch and remaining 1 tablespoon water and mix until cornstarch is dissolved. Slowly pour mixture into berries and stir. Allow to simmer over low heat, while stirring continuously, until mixture is thickened, 1–2 minutes. Remove from heat and set on counter to cool slightly, about 20 minutes.

2. For Chocolate Funnel Cake: In a large shallow pot, heat oil over medium heat to 375°F. Line four large plates with paper towels and set aside.

3. In a large bowl, whisk together egg and milk until frothy, 2 minutes. Add sugar, flour, cocoa powder, salt, and baking powder and whisk until fully combined and no lumps are left, about 2 minutes.

FOR ASSEMBLY

1 (4-ounce) bar white chocolate, cut into thin pieces

2 cups cinnamon crunch cereal

8 tablespoons sweetened condensed milk

4. Take a large food-safe funnel and place your finger over small opening at bottom. Pour ¼ batter into top of funnel. Once oil is at temperature, hold funnel over oil and release your finger to allow batter to flow into oil. Carefully swirl batter to make a single layer about 6" in diameter. Allow Funnel Cake to cook about 1 minute or until underside is no longer wet, flip, and cook an additional 45 seconds or until entire Cake is cooked through and no longer wet. Carefully remove Cake with tongs to prepared plate. Repeat cooking with remaining batter to make three more Cakes.

5. To Assemble: Remove paper towels from under Funnel Cakes and set each Cake on a serving plate. Scoop ¼ Mixed Berry Sauce onto each Funnel Cake. Sprinkle with white chocolate and cinnamon crunch cereal. Drizzle sweetened condensed milk over each Cake and serve immediately.

Trick or Treat Sweets Churros

Churros Cart, New Orleans Square, Halloween

· · · ✦ · · ·

For kids and adults alike, Halloween is all about the *candy*! And one of the most popular candies is the delicious combination of caramel, chocolate, and cookie: the TWIX bar. Disneyland decided to pay homage to trick-or-treating and the famous TWIX bar by creating these loaded churros. Not a fan of TWIX? Don't fret! Just dip into your trick-or-treat bag after Halloween, pick whatever candy you want, and add it to the top of these churros in place of the TWIX.

MAKES 12 CHURROS

FOR CHURROS

1 cup room-temperature water

3 tablespoons granulated sugar

½ teaspoon salt

3 tablespoons vegetable oil

1 cup all-purpose flour

FOR ASSEMBLY

10 (1") shortbread cookies

¼ cup granulated sugar

48 ounces vegetable oil, for frying

¼ cup caramel sauce

¼ cup chocolate sauce

6 tablespoons crushed TWIX candy bar pieces

1. To make Churros: Line a half-sized baking sheet with parchment paper and a plate with a paper towel and set aside.

2. In a medium saucepan over medium-high heat, add water, sugar, salt, and oil. Stir until mixture reaches a boil, about 4 minutes, then remove from heat. Add flour and stir until combined.

3. Scoop dough into a large piping bag fitted with a large star tip or a churro maker fitted with a large star tip. Let dough cool until you are able to hold the bag comfortably, about 3 minutes.

4. Pipe cooled dough in twelve 6" lines onto prepared baking sheet. Place sheet in freezer to set 15 minutes.

5. To Assemble: Place shortbread cookies and sugar in a large zip-top bag and crush with a rolling pin into a fine powder. Pour into a shallow dish and set aside.

6. In a large heavy-bottomed pot over medium-high heat, add oil. (It should measure to a depth of at least 3".) Heat until oil reaches 375°F. Line a large plate with paper towels and set aside.

7. Carefully slide one Churro at a time into hot oil, only frying 3–4 at a time to prevent crowding. Flip while frying until golden brown, about 2 minutes total. Remove from oil with tongs to prepared plate and repeat with remaining eleven Churros.

8. While Churros are still hot, roll them in prepared cookie and sugar coating until covered and place on serving plates. Drizzle with caramel and chocolate sauces and finish with a sprinkling of TWIX pieces. Serve immediately.

Pumpkin Churro Funnel Cake

Hungry Bear Restaurant, Halloween

. . . ✳ . . .

There are a lot of Halloween snack and dessert offerings at the Disneyland Resort during September and October, and all of them are wonderful! But it is always a treat to get something to eat from Hungry Bear Restaurant because it has plenty of tables to go around, versus other Quick Service locations where you'll have to eat your churro on the go.

SERVES 4

FOR FUNNEL CAKES

48 ounces vegetable oil, for frying

1½ cups whole milk

2 large eggs

2 cups all-purpose flour

1 teaspoon baking powder

2 teaspoons ground cinnamon

½ teaspoon salt

FOR ASSEMBLY

½ cup granulated sugar

1 tablespoon ground cinnamon

¼ cup caramel sauce

4 scoops pumpkin spice ice cream

1 cup canned whipped cream

1. To make Funnel Cakes: In a large pot over medium-high heat, add vegetable oil to reach a depth of about 3". Heat until oil reaches 375°F. Line a half-sized baking sheet with paper towels and set aside.

2. In a large bowl, whisk together milk and eggs until well combined. Add flour, baking powder, cinnamon, and salt and whisk to combine. Batter should be slightly thicker than pancake batter.

3. Add ½ cup batter to a funnel or spouted measuring cup, keeping narrow end closed. Starting in center of oil, pour batter slowly from narrow end of funnel while spiraling outward. Cook 3 minutes per side or until golden brown. Remove to paper towel–lined baking sheet. Repeat with remaining batter to make three more Cakes.

4. To Assemble: Combine sugar and cinnamon in a shallow dish and coat each Funnel Cake in mixture while still hot.

5. Transfer Funnel Cakes to serving plates. Drizzle each with caramel sauce and place a large scoop of pumpkin spice ice cream on the center of each Funnel Cake. Finish with two squirts of whipped cream above each ice cream scoop to make Mickey ears. Serve immediately.

Blood Orange Slush

Galactic Grill, Halloween

· · · ✷ · · ·

"I vant to suck your blood!!!" No, it's not the blood that vampires like:
A blood orange is a variety of orange that has a deeper color than a traditional orange.
But the name sure makes it sound like a Halloween treat, and the look is simply
spooky—and stunning. Blood orange syrup may be hard to find at grocery stores but is
easily obtained from online retailers. If you get the chance to sip on
one of these at Disneyland, there is an optional addition of a "poison apple"
glow cube to make the drink even spookier.

SERVES 1

1 ounce puréed raspberry
    sauce
8 ounces blood orange
    syrup
2 ounces club soda
3 cups crushed ice

1. Drizzle the inside of a 16-ounce plastic cup or glass with puréed raspberry sauce and set aside.

2. Add blood orange syrup, club soda, and ice to a blender and blend until smooth. Pour into prepared cup, add a straw, and serve immediately.

Peppermint Hot Chocolate

French Market Restaurant, Christmas

· · · ✳ · · ·

Most times of the year, guests flock to the French Market Restaurant for their Jambalaya and "Po'boy" sandwiches. But during the Christmas season, there is something else drawing the crowds: a cup of rich and creamy Peppermint Hot Chocolate. It is the perfect holiday treat to enjoy while strolling through Disneyland. Pair it with a pile of fluffy beignets, and you'll have a delicious and decadent snack that you'll never forget. At home, you can whip up this recipe any time you want a taste of Christmas.

SERVES 4

$3\frac{1}{2}$ **cups whole milk**

$\frac{1}{3}$ **cup unsweetened cocoa powder**

1 cup granulated sugar

$\frac{1}{8}$ **teaspoon salt**

$\frac{1}{3}$ **cup water**

1 ounce peppermint syrup

$\frac{1}{2}$ **cup half-and-half**

2 cups canned whipped cream

4 teaspoons crushed candy cane pieces

1. Combine milk, cocoa powder, sugar, salt, and water in a medium saucepan over medium heat. Stir continuously until well mixed and hot, 3–5 minutes. Remove from heat and stir in peppermint syrup.

2. Pour into four mugs or foam heat-resistant cups. Top each with half-and-half and swirl on whipped cream. Sprinkle with crushed candy cane and serve immediately.

Peppermint Holiday Sundaes

Gibson Girl Ice Cream Parlor, Christmas

. . . ✴ . . .

Gibson Girl Ice Cream Parlor is named after the fictional character created in the 1890s by Charles Dana Gibson. The parlor serves ice cream all year round but offers special sundaes during various holidays, like this Peppermint Holiday Sundae at Christmastime.

SERVES 4

1 large egg white

2 tablespoons heavy cream

1/4 cup granulated sugar

1/8 teaspoon salt

1/2 teaspoon vanilla extract

1/2 teaspoon almond extract

1/3 cup all-purpose flour

3 tablespoons salted butter, melted

2 cups dark chocolate melting wafers

3 tablespoons crushed candy cane pieces, divided

1 cup hot fudge

6 cups peppermint ice cream

4 cups canned whipped cream

4 maraschino cherries, stem on

1. Preheat waffle cone maker to medium heat.

2. In bowl of a stand mixer fitted with whisk attachment, add egg white and beat on high 2 minutes or until foamy. Add in heavy cream, sugar, salt, and vanilla and almond extracts. Whip 2 minutes more. Add flour and whisk 1 minute more. Slowly add in melted butter while whisking and whip 1 additional minute or until all is combined.

3. Scoop 1/2 cup prepared batter into preheated waffle cone maker. Close and cook 1 minute or until golden brown. Remove and immediately press into a 1-cup heat-resistant bowl and allow to set 5 minutes or until hard. Remove from bowl and set aside. Repeat with remaining batter to make three more bowls.

4. Place melting wafers in a medium microwave-safe bowl and microwave on half power for 30 seconds and stir. Repeat until wafers are melted and chocolate is smooth. Dip waffle bowl top edges in chocolate or spread on top edges using a knife. While chocolate is still liquid, sprinkle on some of 2 tablespoons candy cane pieces. Repeat with remaining three waffle bowls and place in freezer to harden 30 minutes.

5. Spoon hot fudge into bottom of waffle bowls, scoop in ice cream, and top each sundae with a swirl of whipped cream, some of the remaining 1 tablespoon candy cane pieces, and a maraschino cherry.

Christmas Punch

Galactic Grill, Christmas

· · · ✦ · · ·

Holiday cheer bursts in every sip of this vibrant punch! Pomegranate, cranberry, and orange sing a familiar melody on your tongue, each note dancing with nostalgia for snowy days and twinkling lights. More than just a drink, it's a festive feast for the eyes. Ruby arils, crimson cranberries, and orange slices float like ornaments, and a sprig of rosemary mimics a fir branch from a Christmas tree. Though the Christmas Fantasy Parade doesn't pass the Galactic Grill, worry not! It is just a few steps to Main Street U.S.A., where you can enjoy your punch while seeing live toy soldiers march by.

SERVES 1

½ cup cranberry juice

½ cup pulp-free orange juice

¼ cup pomegranate juice

½ cup lemon-lime soda

1 half-wheel fresh orange

¼ cup fresh cranberries

1 sprig fresh rosemary

1. In a 16-ounce plastic cup or glass, add cranberry juice, orange juice, and pomegranate juice and stir to combine. Pour in lemon-lime soda and add ice to top cup.

2. Garnish with orange wheel, cranberries, and rosemary sprig on top of ice. Serve immediately.

Serving Tip

If you're making this punch for a party, try making it in bulk in a pitcher or drink dispenser with all the garnishes set off to the side in separate bowls. Then guests can adorn their drink however they like!

Mickey Gingerbread

Jolly Holiday Bakery Cafe, Christmas

· · · · ✳ · · ·

Ah, the Mickey Gingerbread cookie—a Disneyland legend! This spiced marvel is so popular that Disney bakes up a "Halfway to the Holidays" batch in June just to soothe guest cravings. Disneyland gives the cookies an outline in white; green buttons down the center; a red bowtie; black eyes, nose, and mouth; and pink cheeks. But feel free to decorate them as you'd like!

MAKES 12 COOKIES

½ cup salted butter

½ cup dark brown sugar

3 tablespoons molasses

1¾ cups all-purpose flour

1 tablespoon ground ginger

1 teaspoon ground cinnamon

½ teaspoon baking soda

2 tablespoons half-and-half

12 tablespoons premade white cookie icing

12 teaspoons premade black cookie icing

6 teaspoons premade red cookie icing

6 teaspoons premade green cookie icing

3 teaspoons premade pink cookie icing

1. In bowl of a stand mixer fitted with paddle attachment, cream together butter and brown sugar at medium speed 2 minutes or until creamy. Add in molasses and stir 1 minute more. Gradually add in flour while running mixer on low speed until all flour is added and well combined.

2. Add in ginger, cinnamon, baking soda, and half-and-half and mix 2 minutes or until well combined. Flatten into a ½"-thick disk, wrap in plastic wrap, and chill 1 hour in refrigerator.

3. Preheat oven to 375°F and line a full-sized baking sheet with parchment paper. Set aside.

4. Remove dough disk from refrigerator and sandwich between two sheets of parchment paper. Use a rolling pin to roll dough out to ¼" thickness, cut out 12 Mickey shapes, and place on prepared baking sheet. Bake 10–12 minutes until bottoms brown and tops no longer look puffy. Remove from oven and allow cookies to cool on pan 30 minutes.

5. Once Mickeys are totally cooled, decorate with premade icing as desired. Allow icing to dry and harden 30 minutes, then enjoy. Leftover cookies can be kept at room temperature in a sealed container up to 1 week.

Caldo de Pollo

. . . ✳ . . .

Caldo de pollo, meaning "chicken broth" in Spanish, is the name of a hearty chicken soup popular in Mexico. It's a comforting dish packed with chicken and vegetables, including a chunk of an ear of corn! The predominant religion of Mexico is Roman Catholicism, so Christmas is a huge holiday celebrated across the country. Share a large pot of this soup with loved ones during the chilly Christmas season. The simmering soup will have you feeling cozy and toasty in no time.

SERVES 6

2 tablespoons vegetable oil, divided

2 boneless skinless chicken thighs, cubed

1 small yellow onion, peeled and diced

2 medium carrots, peeled and diced

2 medium stalks celery, diced

3 medium Yukon gold potatoes, peeled and diced

1 teaspoon chili powder

1 teaspoon ground cumin

1 teaspoon dried oregano

1 teaspoon ground coriander

1. In a large pot over medium heat, add 1 tablespoon oil and heat 3 minutes. Add chicken and stir to sear, about 5 minutes. Remove chicken from pot.

2. Add remaining 1 tablespoon oil to same pot at medium heat, and then add onion. Cook 3 minutes, stirring frequently. Add in carrots, celery, potatoes, and all seasonings. Cook 3 minutes. Add in garlic and cook 2 minutes more.

3. Return chicken to pot and add tomatoes, green chilies, and chicken broth. Bring to a boil, reduce heat to low, and cook uncovered 20 minutes or until chicken is cooked through.

½ teaspoon paprika

½ teaspoon salt

¼ teaspoon ground black pepper

3 teaspoons minced garlic

1 (15-ounce) can fire roasted tomatoes, including juices

2 tablespoons mild diced green chilies

36 ounces chicken broth

2 ears sweet corn, cut into thirds

2 cups pre-cooked white rice

½ cup chopped fresh cilantro

1 lime, cut into wedges

4. Add corn and rice to the pot and simmer another 10 minutes or until corn is cooked. Ladle into six soup bowls, making sure each bowl has a chunk of corn. Garnish with a sprinkle of cilantro and a lime wedge each and serve immediately. Leftovers can be refrigerated in an airtight container up to 4 days.

CHAPTER 4

Magic Kingdom

Magic Kingdom truly shines during spooky season and the winter holidays, hosting both Mickey's Not-So-Scary Halloween Party and Mickey's Very Merry Christmas Party. The Park's transformation between these events seems impossibly swift—most of the magic happens in just one night! Within a week, the landscape shifts from grinning jack-o-lanterns to twinkling snowflakes, creating an experience some guests plan their entire trip around. Meticulous planning, logistical expertise, and dedicated Cast Members make this seemingly instantaneous decorating feat happen.

As you might expect, recipes in this chapter therefore lean heavily toward Halloween and Christmas favorites (with a nod to the Fourth of July via Berry Shortcake!)—inspired by the Park's stellar seasonal parties. Dive into the ultra-popular Almond Sweet Corn Cake from Pecos Bill Tall Tale Inn and Cafe, indulge in the Binx Pastry Tails from Cheshire Café, or whip up a super-sweet Sugar Plum Shake from Auntie Gravity's Galactic Goodies. Bring the party home and experience the wonder of Disney's Magic Kingdom through these delicious treats!

FRONTIERLAND

LIBERTY SQUARE

1

4

10

5 12

9

7

ADVENTURELAND

MAIN STREET U.S.A.

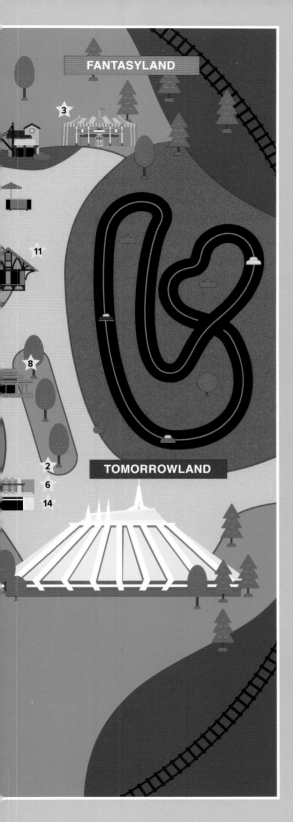

MAGIC KINGDOM

1   **BERRY SHORTCAKE**
(Columbia Harbour House, Fourth of July)

2   **NOT-SO-POISON APPLE PIE MILK SHAKE**
(Auntie Gravity's Galactic Goodies, Halloween)

3   **PUMPKIN FUDGE**
(Big Top Souvenirs, Halloween)

4   **THE DOOM BERRY**
(Sleepy Hollow, Halloween)

5   **SPELLBINDING FRIED PIES**
(Golden Oak Outpost, Halloween)

6   **SWEET CORN AND VANILLA SOFT-SERVE SWIRLS**
(Auntie Gravity's Galactic Goodies, Halloween)

7   **PAIN AND PANIC HOT DOG**
(Casey's Corner, Halloween)

8   **RIVER STYX ELIXIR**
(Cosmic Ray's Starlight Cafe, Halloween)

9   **ALMOND SWEET CORN CAKE**
(Pecos Bill Tall Tale Inn and Cafe, Halloween)

10   **UN POCO LOCO TOTS**
(The Friar's Nook, Halloween)

11   **BINX PASTRY TAILS**
(Cheshire Café, Halloween)

12   **CHAI-CARAMEL FREEZE**
(Golden Oak Outpost, Christmas)

13   **CHRISTMAS WREATH DOUGHNUTS**
(Snack Carts on Main Street U.S.A., Christmas)

14   **SUGAR PLUM SHAKE**
(Auntie Gravity's Galactic Goodies, Christmas)

Berry Shortcake

Columbia Harbour House, Fourth of July

. . . ✦ . . .

The Fourth of July is one of the busiest days at the Magic Kingdom. To please the plethora of guests, Disney pulls out all the stops to display one of the largest fireworks shows in the world, with over fifteen thousand fireworks shells lighting up the sky. This Berry Shortcake is bursting with fresh, sweet flavor and offers a colorful presentation of its own. The following recipe makes a whole pan, so plan on bringing it to your Fourth of July barbecue each year!

SERVES 20

1 cup salted butter, softened

3¼ cups granulated sugar, divided

6 large eggs

3 cups all-purpose flour

½ cup heavy whipping cream

½ cup sour cream

1 tablespoon vanilla extract

10 cups hulled and quartered fresh strawberries

10 cups fresh blueberries

1 (13-ounce) can extra-creamy whipped cream

⅓ cup red, white, and blue star sprinkles

1. Preheat oven to 325°F. Spray a 9" × 13" glass pan with baking spray and set aside.

2. In bowl of a stand mixer fitted with paddle attachment, add butter and 3 cups sugar and beat on low 1 minute or until well combined. Add in eggs one at a time while beating, and beat 1 minute more after each egg addition. Add in flour, whipping cream, sour cream, and vanilla extract and mix 2 minutes or until well combined.

3. Smooth mixture into prepared baking pan and bake 55–65 minutes until knife inserted in center comes out clean. Remove from oven and allow to cool completely in pan, about 45 minutes. Cut into 20 rectangles.

4. Place strawberries and blueberries in a large bowl and sprinkle on remaining ¼ cup sugar. Mix well.

5. To serve, scoop 1 cup mixed berries into bottom of a serving bowl. Add a slice of cake and top with a large squirt of whipped cream. Top with red, white, and blue sprinkles and eat immediately. Mixed berries are fresh the day they are served; leftover cake can be covered in plastic wrap and stored at room temperature up to 3 days.

Not-So-Poison
Apple Pie Milk Shake

Auntie Gravity's Galactic Goodies, Halloween

· · · ✳ · · ·

The "poison apple" made famous by Walt Disney's first full-length feature film, *Snow White and the Seven Dwarfs*, shows up in a chilling scene of the disguised evil queen poisoning Snow White with an innocent-looking apple. Luckily, this treat has no poison in it whatsoever and is just dripping with deliciousness. Only offered during Mickey's Not-So-Scary Halloween Party at Magic Kingdom, you can enjoy this at home without an extra entrance ticket! If you're looking to save a bit of time, swap the homemade pumpkin marshmallow decor with a large marshmallow round and use edible markers to give it a scary grin.

SERVES 1

FOR MARSHMALLOW DECOR

¾ **cup water, divided**
3 **(0.25-ounce) packets unflavored gelatin**
⅔ **cup light corn syrup**
2 **cups granulated sugar**
1 **teaspoon vanilla paste**
5 **drops green gel food coloring**
¼ **cup cornstarch**
¼ **cup confectioners' sugar**

1. To make Marshmallow Decor: Prepare twelve silicone pumpkin molds with a thin layer of nonstick cooking spray and set aside.

2. In bowl of a stand mixer fitted with whisk attachment, add ½ cup water, sprinkle gelatin on top of water, and let sit 5 minutes.

3. Meanwhile, combine remaining ¼ cup water, corn syrup, granulated sugar, and vanilla paste in a small saucepan. Over medium heat, bring mixture to a boil and allow to boil 1 minute, stirring frequently.

4. Remove from heat and gently pour into stand mixer while mixing slowly until entire saucepan is emptied. Raise mixer speed to high and mix 12 minutes or until fluffy and stiff peaks form. Stir in green food coloring until color is well incorporated.

(continued) ▶

FOR MILK SHAKE

3 cups vanilla ice cream

¼ cup whole milk

2 ounces Monin Granny Apple Syrup

½ teaspoon pumpkin pie spice

FOR WHIPPED CREAM TOPPING

½ cup heavy whipping cream

1 tablespoon confectioners' sugar

1 tablespoon Monin Granny Apple Syrup

FOR ASSEMBLY

2 cinnamon doughnut holes

5. Pour Marshmallow into prepared pumpkin molds until each mold is full. Grease a piece of plastic wrap with nonstick cooking spray and smooth over top of each fluff. Allow to sit at room temperature 3 hours up to overnight.

6. After set, carefully slide each Marshmallow out of its container. Combine cornstarch and confectioners' sugar in a shallow bowl and roll each Marshmallow in mixture. Dust off excess. Set one fluff aside for this recipe, and store the rest in an airtight container at room temperature up to 3 days.

7. To make Milk Shake: Add ice cream, milk, syrup, and pumpkin pie spice to a blender. Blend 1–2 minutes until smooth and creamy. Pour into plastic or glass 18-ounce cup and set in freezer.

8. To make Whipped Cream Topping: In bowl of a stand mixer fitted with whisk attachment, add whipping cream and sugar. Whip on high speed until stiff peaks form. Add in syrup and stir until combined.

9. To Assemble: Remove Milk Shake from freezer and scoop Whipped Cream Topping on top. Add in a large-gauge straw and place one pumpkin Marshmallow Decor on top, along with cinnamon doughnut holes. Serve immediately.

Serving Tip

Looks like you've got eleven extra pumpkin marshmallows! These will make a delicious garnish to any Halloween dessert you cook up over the holiday, including brownies, cookies, or a bowl of ice cream.

Pumpkin Fudge

Big Top Souvenirs, Halloween

. . . ✳ . . .

Big Top Souvenirs is tucked into Storybook Circus in Fantasyland at Magic Kingdom. Here you will find display cases brimming with seasonal and mainstay treats and sweets that are always a perfect addition to your day. There is even seating under a circus tent where you can park your crew and eat your confections. And while Pumpkin Fudge can only be bought at Big Top during the autumn months, you can make it at home any time of year!

SERVES 16

¾ cup salted butter

¾ cup heavy whipping cream

1½ cups granulated sugar

¼ cup pumpkin purée

1 teaspoon pumpkin pie spice

1 (11-ounce) package white chocolate chips

1 (7-ounce) jar marshmallow creme

5 drops orange gel food coloring

1. Line an 8" × 8" glass or metal pan with parchment paper and set aside.

2. In a large pan over medium heat, add butter, whipping cream, sugar, pumpkin purée, and pumpkin pie spice. Stir until well combined and allow to come to a boil. Stirring frequently, bring mixture to 237°F, then remove from heat.

3. While mixture is still hot, whisk in white chocolate chips, marshmallow creme, and food coloring. Pour into prepared baking pan and refrigerate to set at least 5 hours up to overnight.

4. Cut into squares to serve. Leftovers can be covered and refrigerated in pan up to 1 week.

The Doom Berry

Sleepy Hollow, Halloween

· · · ✦ · · ·

"Doom Berry" is a riff on the Haunted Mansion ride vehicle name "Doom Buggy." But there's nothing to fear here: Ginger ale and blackberry go great together and provide a refreshing beverage when you're out trick-or-treating all night! The luster dust adds a fun look but no actual flavor, so you can keep it or omit it. Sleepy Hollow is a snack window at the edge of Liberty Square in Magic Kingdom, and the name refers to the fictional town in the Disney animated film *The Legend of Sleepy Hollow* featuring Ichabod Crane and the Headless Horseman.

SERVES 1

7.5 ounces ginger ale
1 ounce blackberry purée
⅛ teaspoon edible silver luster dust
1 large fresh mint leaf

In a 16-ounce plastic or glass cup, add ginger ale, blackberry purée, and luster dust. Stir to combine. Top with ice until cup is full, add a straw, place mint leaf on top of ice, and enjoy.

Disney Parks Tip

Sleepy Hollow is located near Cinderella Castle, over the bridge into Liberty Square. During Mickey's Not-So-Scary Halloween Party, the Boo-To-You Parade passes right over that bridge—making the area around Sleepy Hollow a perfect place to view the parade! Grab this drink and a snack and stake your spot.

Spellbinding Fried Pies

Golden Oak Outpost, Halloween

· · · ✦ · · ·

Inspired by the magical book from the movie *Hocus Pocus*, this fried pie allows you to hold the power of witches in your hands. Careful not to look too closely into its eye, though, you never know what might happen! The exclusive food and beverage items offered at Mickey's Not-So-Scary Halloween Party tend to lean toward the sweet side, so snagging this savory bite is a must to offset all that candy!

MAKES 4 PIES

FOR FRIED PIES
- **48 ounces vegetable oil, for frying**
- **1 cup shredded cooked chicken**
- **¼ cup shredded mozzarella cheese**
- **2 tablespoons blue cheese crumbles**
- **2 tablespoons Buffalo sauce**
- **1 (14.1-ounce) 2-pack refrigerated pie dough, room temperature**

1. Pour oil in a large shallow pot or Dutch oven and place over medium heat. Bring temperature to 375°F.

2. To make Fried Pies: In a medium bowl, mix together chicken, mozzarella cheese, blue cheese, and Buffalo sauce. Set aside.

3. Roll out pie doughs carefully and cut out 4 (3" × 2") rectangles from each dough circle for 8 total rectangles. Discard excess. Scoop ¼ chicken filling onto center of one rectangle, wet a finger in water, and run finger around the outside edge, then place a clean dough rectangle on top of chicken filling. Use a fork to press and crimp edges to seal. Repeat with remaining dough and filling to make 4 Pies.

4. Once oil is at 375°F, carefully lower up to 2 Pies in hot oil and fry 2–5 minutes per side until crust is cooked and browned. Remove from oil to a paper towel–lined plate and repeat with remaining Pies.

(continued) ▶

FOR JALAPEÑO-RANCH AÏOLI

½ **cup sour cream**

2 **tablespoons chopped fresh cilantro**

1 **tablespoon chopped seeded jalapeño**

1 **teaspoon lime juice**

½ **teaspoon salt**

½ **teaspoon onion powder**

½ **teaspoon garlic powder**

FOR ASSEMBLY

4 **large candy eyeballs**

5. To make Jalapeño-Ranch Aïoli: Add all ingredients to a food processor or blender and blend 1–2 minutes until well combined and creamy. Set aside.

6. To Assemble: When Pies are cooled enough to eat (about 15 minutes), drizzle Aïoli on top and place one candy eye on each Pie. Serve immediately.

Serving Tip

If you want to make these pies for a crowd, take orders and adjust the filling to each guest's preferences. Omit the Buffalo sauce and sub with barbecue sauce, or try plant-based meats instead of chicken. Whatever fillings you and your guests decide on, you can bet your party will be **magic***!*

Sweet Corn and Vanilla Soft-Serve Swirls

Auntie Gravity's Galactic Goodies, Halloween

· · · ✳ · · ·

Perhaps most people don't scour the freezers at their local grocery store looking for Sweet Corn and Vanilla Soft-Serve, but that's what makes this chilled treat so endearing—it's original and unexpected! The flavor will surprise you, with the familiar taste of corn but also the sweetness of vanilla. It's the perfect trick *and* treat that complements any Halloween party at home.

SERVES 2

1 tablespoon cream
  cheese, softened
1/3 cup granulated sugar
1 teaspoon vanilla extract
3/4 cup heavy whipping
  cream
1 cup whole milk
1 cup canned sweet corn,
  drained

1. In a large bowl, whisk together cream cheese, sugar, and vanilla until well combined. Add in whipping cream and milk, stirring continuously, until fully incorporated. Pour corn into mixture and refrigerate 2 hours up to overnight.

2. Pour mixture through a tight mesh sieve and discard corn. Run in an ice cream machine according to manufacturer's instructions until smooth and creamy.

3. Scoop into bowls and enjoy immediately, or store leftovers in freezer up to 1 week.

Pain and Panic Hot Dog

Casey's Corner, Halloween

· · · ✳ · · ·

This hot dog is named after the slapstick duo Pain and Panic, who are the minions of Hades in the Disney movie *Hercules*. Casey's Corner is always serving up hot and fresh hot dogs on Main Street U.S.A., but only during Halloween time can you snag this devil of a meal. Grab one to split with your friends while watching Disney's Not-So-Spooky Spectacular Halloween Fireworks light up the sky above Cinderella Castle.

SERVES 1

FOR SWEET AND SPICY ONION RELISH

1 medium sweet onion, peeled and diced
1 tablespoon salted butter
1 tablespoon light brown sugar
1 tablespoon balsamic vinegar
1 tablespoon red wine vinegar
¼ teaspoon salt

FOR ASSEMBLY

1 (6") beef frank
1 hot dog bun
2 tablespoons crushed Flamin' Hot Cheetos
1 tablespoon sriracha mayo

1. To make Sweet and Spicy Onion Relish: Sauté onion and butter in a large skillet over medium-low heat 10 minutes or until brown and caramelized. Add brown sugar and stir. Add in balsamic and red wine vinegars and salt and stir. Continue cooking and stirring about 10 minutes more or until most of the liquid has evaporated.

2. Scoop Relish into a small bowl and refrigerate until ready to use. Excess can be refrigerated in an airtight container up to 1 week.

3. To Assemble: Place beef frank in hot dog bun and top with Sweet and Spicy Onion Relish, crushed Flamin' Hot Cheetos, and sriracha mayo. Serve immediately.

Serving Tip

At home, you can adjust the "pain" and "panic" levels by adding more or less Flamin' Hot Cheetos and sriracha mayo.

River Styx Elixir

Cosmic Ray's Starlight Cafe, Halloween

· · · ✦ · · ·

In Greek mythology, the River Styx is how the dead are brought to Hades's realm. In the
Disney movie *Hercules*, a young woman named Megara is dropped into the River Styx
by Hades. Hercules is able to rescue her, but it's still pretty creepy, huh?
Well, that makes this a perfect beverage for spooky season both
at Magic Kingdom and your home.

SERVES 1

8 ounces lemonade
2 ounces kiwi syrup
¼ teaspoon silver luster dust

Pour lemonade, kiwi syrup, and luster dust into a cocktail shaker
half full of ice, seal, and shake well. Pour into a 16-ounce plastic
cup or glass and fill to top with ice. Serve immediately.

Almond Sweet Corn Cake

Pecos Bill Tall Tale Inn and Cafe, Halloween

· · · ✦ · · ·

It's corn! It's a cake! It's an almond-vanilla-flavored, corn-shaped cake! These sweets have been so popular at Mickey's Not-So-Scary Halloween Party that they typically sell out within the first hour of the party. Instead of racing to Pecos Bill, you can make these easily at home. If you don't have a corn-shaped pan, you can get one at online retailers. Now you can have your cake...and your corn too!

SERVES 4

FOR ALMOND-VANILLA CAKE

4 large egg yolks

½ cup granulated sugar

1½ cups almond flour

1 teaspoon vanilla extract

1 teaspoon almond extract

4 drops orange gel food coloring

FOR ASSEMBLY

4 tablespoons white icing

4 tablespoons orange icing

½ cup candy corn

1. To make Almond-Vanilla Cake: Preheat oven to 350°F. Lightly grease a corn-shaped mold with nonstick cooking spray and set aside.

2. In bowl of a stand mixer fitted with paddle attachment, add egg yolks and sugar. Mix 1–2 minutes until creamy. Add in almond flour, vanilla extract, and almond extract. Mix until combined and no flour pockets remain. Add in orange food coloring and mix until color is consistent throughout.

3. Pour batter into prepared corn pan and bake 12–15 minutes until a knife inserted in center comes out clean. Remove from oven and allow to cool in pan 10 minutes, then invert onto a cooling rack to cool completely, about 1 hour.

4. To Assemble: Place Cake on a serving plate and drizzle with white and orange icings, then top with candy corn. Serve immediately or refrigerate in an airtight container up to 2 days.

Un Poco Loco Tots

The Friar's Nook, Halloween

· · · ✦ · · ·

These tots are named after the song "Un Poco Loco" from the Pixar movie *Coco*, which takes place in the land of the dead on the Day of the Dead (Día de los Muertos). Disney serves these tots at about a medium spice level, but at home, you can adjust the spice to exactly your liking. The Friar's Nook is a great place to find specialty tots any time, but these Loco Tots are only available in the fall!

SERVES 1

2 cups cooked potato tots

2 tablespoons cooked chorizo sausage

½ cup nacho cheese sauce

3 teaspoons hot sauce

1 tablespoon chopped green onions

Place tots in a medium bowl and sprinkle with chorizo sausage. In a small bowl, mix together nacho cheese and hot sauce. Drizzle cheese sauce over tots and sausage and finish with chopped green onions on top. Serve immediately.

Binx Pastry Tails

Cheshire Café, Halloween

. . .   ✷   . . .

A "twist" on the classic Cheshire Cat Tail usually served at Cheshire Café, this ode to the boy in *Hocus Pocus* who is cursed to live as a cat adds dark chocolate and a cute Binx chocolate piece. At home, you can omit this edible printed decoration.

SERVES 6

FOR PASTRIES

1 (3.4-ounce) package instant vanilla pudding

1¾ cups whole milk

1 (17.3-ounce) 2-count box frozen puff pastry sheets, thawed

1 cup mini semisweet chocolate chips

1 large egg

1 tablespoon water

FOR TOPPING

1 cup confectioners' sugar

¼ cup heavy cream

1 teaspoon vanilla extract

2 drops purple gel food coloring

½ cup dark chocolate melting wafers

1. To make Pastries: Preheat oven to 400°F. Line a half-sized baking sheet with parchment paper and set aside.

2. In a medium bowl, whisk together pudding and milk. Cover and refrigerate until ready to use, at least 10 minutes.

3. Unfold both puff pastry sheets and use a rolling pin to barely soften each surface. Don't overwork. Spread a very thin layer of vanilla pudding onto each sheet and sprinkle one sheet with mini chocolate chips. Carefully lay other sheet pudding-side down onto chocolate chips.

4. Cut filled pastry into 6 long strips. Holding a strip in your hand, twist one end twice. Lay on prepared baking sheet and repeat with remaining 5 strips. In a small bowl, beat egg and water together. Brush over top of Pastries. Bake 20 minutes or until pastry is golden brown. Allow to cool completely on baking sheet, about 45 minutes.

5. To make Topping: In a small bowl, combine confectioners' sugar, cream, and vanilla. Add in purple food coloring until it reaches desired tone. In a separate, small microwave-safe bowl, place dark chocolate melting wafers. Microwave on half power 30 seconds and stir. Repeat until wafers just melt.

6. Once Pastries are cooled, drizzle each with purple frosting and melted dark chocolate. Serve immediately or refrigerate in an airtight container up to 2 days.

Chai-Caramel Freeze

Golden Oak Outpost, Christmas

. . . ✦ . . .

Chai spices—cinnamon, cardamom, allspice, cloves, nutmeg—really elicit the warmth of the holidays and add a delicious touch to this caramel freeze. The decorative chocolate on top is optional to include at home, but the shape may look familiar to you: It is that of an upside-down gingerbread man! Cooks at Disney were able to repurpose the gingerbread man shape to make a reindeer.

SERVES 1

FOR SALTED CARAMEL FREEZE

3 cups crushed ice

3 ounces caramel sauce

1 ounce cold water

¼ teaspoon salt

FOR CHAI-SPICED WHIPPED CREAM

1 cup heavy whipping cream

2 tablespoons confectioners' sugar

¼ teaspoon ground cinnamon

⅛ teaspoon ground cardamom

1/16 teaspoon ground allspice

1/16 teaspoon ground cloves

1/16 teaspoon ground nutmeg

FOR ASSEMBLY

1 chocolate gingerbread man cookie

Edible paints in white, red, and green

1. To make Salted Caramel Freeze: Place crushed ice, caramel sauce, water, and salt in a blender and blend until smooth. Pour into a 16-ounce plastic cup or glass and set in freezer while making Whipped Cream.

2. To make Chai-Spiced Whipped Cream: In bowl of a stand mixer fitted with whisk attachment, add whipping cream and sugar and whip on high until stiff peaks form, 2–4 minutes. In a small bowl, mix together all chai spices, then pour them into the whipped cream, mixing until just incorporated.

3. To Assemble: Remove Freeze from freezer and scoop Chai-Spiced Whipped Cream on top. Turn chocolate gingerbread man upside down and use edible paints to decorate it to look like a reindeer. Place cookie on whipped cream. Serve immediately.

Christmas Wreath Doughnuts

Snack Carts on Main Street U.S.A., Christmas

. . . ✳ . . .

You'll have to resist the urge to grab these doughnuts and hang them on your door: They are just that festive! Instead of the typical gingerbread house decorating, how about Christmas Wreath Doughnut decorating? Give everyone a plain doughnut and provide lots of frostings and sprinkles to choose from.

MAKES 6 DOUGHNUTS

FOR DOUGHNUTS

- 1 (15.25-ounce) box red velvet cake mix
- 1 cup water
- ½ cup vegetable oil
- 3 large eggs

FOR FROSTING

- ½ cup salted butter, softened
- 2 teaspoons vanilla extract
- 2 cups confectioners' sugar
- 1 tablespoon whole milk
- 5 drops green gel food coloring

FOR ASSEMBLY

- 6 teaspoons assorted Christmas sprinkles

1. Preheat oven to 350°F. Grease a six-divot doughnut pan with nonstick cooking spray and set aside.

2. To make Doughnuts: In bowl of a stand mixer fitted with paddle attachment, add red velvet cake mix, water, vegetable oil, and eggs. Mix until there are no longer pockets of dry mix. Scoop into a piping bag and pipe into prepared doughnut pan. (Discard or bake excess batter in a cupcake pan 19–23 minutes until a knife inserted in center comes out clean.)

3. Bake Doughnuts 15–18 minutes until a knife inserted comes out clean. Remove from oven and allow to cool in the pan on the counter 10 minutes. Carefully invert onto a wire rack to continue to cool fully, about 45 minutes.

4. To make Frosting: In clean bowl of a stand mixer fitted with whisk attachment, add butter, vanilla, sugar, milk, and food coloring. Whip until frosting is uniform in color and light and fluffy. Scoop into a piping bag fitted with a star tip and set aside.

5. To Assemble: Using the star tip to create a leafy effect, pipe Frosting onto the tops of cooled Doughnuts, and then top with sprinkles. Serve immediately. Leftover Doughnuts can be refrigerated in an airtight container up to 2 days.

Sugar Plum Shake

Auntie Gravity's Galactic Goodies, Christmas

. . . ✦ . . .

After making this drink, you may be having visions of Sugar Plum Shakes dancing in your head throughout the holiday season. The flavored syrups can be bought at online retailers and used later in your coffee bar to add to a morning cup of joe or a festive hot chocolate.

SERVES 1

1 ounce Monin Pomegranate Syrup

1 ounce Monin Spiced Brown Sugar Syrup

3 cups vanilla ice cream

¼ cup whole milk

½ cup canned whipped cream

1 tablespoon cherry syrup

1 teaspoon purple sugar sprinkles

1. In a pitcher or blender, add both flavored syrups, ice cream, and milk. Blend until combined and creamy, about 1–2 minutes. Pour into plastic or glass 16-ounce cup.

2. Top with whipped cream, drizzle with cherry syrup, and finish with sugar sprinkles. Enjoy immediately.

Cooking Hack

If you find this shake too sweet, try adjusting the syrup amounts to create the Sugar Plum Shake flavor you desire.

CHAPTER 5

EPCOT

EPCOT is well-known for their International Festival of the Holidays, which turns the World Showcase into a Christmas and Hanukkah marketplace filled with foods and drinks that honor holiday celebrations around the globe. Small pop-up booths have limited-time menus just for the festival. Now you can bring these limited-time offerings into your home each and every year!

While this chapter does include a few popular recipes for Valentine's Day, St. Patrick's Day, the Fourth of July, and Thanksgiving, the bulk of the chapter is focused on Christmas and Hanukkah, particularly Hanukkah, as EPCOT is the only Park to really showcase this Jewish holiday. Favorite treats include the Black and White Cookies, made famous in New York City, along with Sufganiyot doughnuts and warming Chicken and Matzo Ball Soup. Other festive fare offered seasonally in the Park includes St. Patrick's Day Irish Coffee Tarts, Turkey Poutine, and Maple Bûche de Noël. Sink your teeth into the celebratory flavors of EPCOT by whipping up these dishes to share with friends and family.

GERMANY

ITALY

WORLD
SHOWCASE

CHINA

NORWAY

MEXICO

5

WORLD CELEBRATION

6

WORLD DISCOVERY

3

ENTRANCE

EPCOT

1 FLOURLESS CHOCOLATE CAKE
(Coral Reef Restaurant, Valentine's Day)

2 ST. PATRICK'S DAY IRISH COFFEE TARTS
(Sunshine Seasons, St. Patrick's Day)

3 FOURTH OF JULY LIEGE WAFFLE
(Connections Café, Fourth of July)

4 TURKEY POUTINE
(Refreshment Port, Thanksgiving)

5 CHOCOLATE PEPPERMINT SHAKE
(Holiday Sweets & Treats, Christmas)

6 MAPLE BÛCHE DE NOËL
(Holiday Hearth Desserts, Christmas)

7 PASTRAMI ON RYE
(L'Chaim! Holiday Kitchen, Hanukkah)

8 SMOKED SALMON POTATO LATKES
(L'Chaim! Holiday Kitchen, Hanukkah)

9 SUFGANIYOT
(L'Chaim! Holiday Kitchen, Hanukkah)

10 BLACK AND WHITE COOKIES
(L'Chaim! Holiday Kitchen, Hanukkah)

11 CHICKEN AND MATZO BALL SOUP
(L'Chaim! Holiday Kitchen, Hanukkah)

12 POTATO KNISH
(L'Chaim! Holiday Kitchen, Hanukkah)

13 EGG CREAM
(L'Chaim! Holiday Kitchen, Hanukkah)

Flourless Chocolate Cake

Coral Reef Restaurant, Valentine's Day

. . . ✦ . . .

This cake doesn't sacrifice any flavor without the flour. In fact, this may be the moistest cake you've ever had, and the pop of raspberry does a great job adding depth of flavor and a hint of freshness to complement the cake and set the Valentine's Day mood. Coral Reef Restaurant draws people in with its 5.7-million-gallon saltwater aquarium that is home to over two thousand sea creatures—which you can see from your dining table! Now you can enjoy this dessert at home with your Valentine.

MAKES 10 CAKES

FOR MERINGUES

2 large egg whites
$1/8$ teaspoon cream of tartar
$1/8$ teaspoon salt
$1/3$ cup granulated sugar

FOR CHOCOLATE CAKES

1 cup semisweet chocolate chips
$1/2$ cup salted butter, softened
$3/4$ cup granulated sugar
$1/4$ teaspoon salt
1 teaspoon vanilla extract
3 large eggs
$1/2$ cup cocoa powder

1. To make Meringues: Preheat oven to 225°F. Line a half-sized baking sheet with parchment paper and set aside.

2. In bowl of a stand mixer fitted with whisk attachment, add egg whites, cream of tartar, and salt and beat until soft peaks form, about 3–5 minutes. Gradually add sugar, whipping until stiff peaks form, about 8–10 minutes.

3. Scoop into a large piping bag fitted with a medium star tip and pipe 20 ($1/2$"-diameter) dollops onto prepared baking sheet. Bake 2 hours or until crisp and dry. Allow to cool 30 minutes on pan to complete hardening. Carefully remove from pan and set aside.

4. To make Chocolate Cakes: Preheat oven to 375°F and thoroughly grease a silicone bar mold ($4\frac{1}{2}$" × $1\frac{1}{2}$" cavities) with nonstick cooking spray. Set aside.

(continued) ▶

FOR CHOCOLATE GLAZE

1 cup dark chocolate chips

½ cup heavy whipping cream

FOR RASPBERRY WHIPPED CREAM

1 cup heavy whipping cream

¼ cup confectioners' sugar

½ teaspoon raspberry extract

1 drop red gel food coloring

FOR WHITE CHOCOLATE DECORATIONS

1 cup white chocolate chips

5 drops red gel food coloring

5. Place chocolate chips and butter in a large microwave-safe bowl and microwave 1 minute. Stir until all chips melt. Stir in sugar, salt, and vanilla. Allow to cool 5 minutes, then add eggs and cocoa powder and stir until just combined, about 1 minute.

6. Spoon batter into prepared molds and bake 20–25 minutes until a knife inserted in center comes out clean. Remove from oven and allow to cool completely in the molds, about 30 minutes. Carefully remove from molds onto a wire rack.

7. To make Chocolate Glaze: Place chocolate chips and heavy cream in a medium microwave-safe bowl, microwave 1 minute, and stir until all chips are melted. Once Cakes are completely cool, pour Glaze over Cakes to coat. Allow Glaze to set 10 minutes.

8. To make Raspberry Whipped Cream: In bowl of a stand mixer fitted with whisk attachment, add whipping cream, sugar, raspberry extract, and food coloring and whip on high speed 5–7 minutes until stiff peaks form. Scoop into a large piping bag fitted with a medium circle tip and set aside.

9. To make White Chocolate Decorations: Line a half-sized baking sheet with parchment paper and set aside. In a small microwave-safe bowl, add white chocolate chips and microwave in 30-second increments, stirring between each, until chips just melt. Add food coloring and stir to combine. Using a spatula, smooth chocolate into a single (⅛") layer across prepared baking sheet. Place in freezer to set 30 minutes.

FOR ASSEMBLY

10 tablespoons raspberry jam

30 fresh raspberries

5 teaspoons edible gold leaf

10. Once chocolate is set, fill a medium bowl with hot water and place a knife and a 1" heart cookie cutter in hot water. Remove cookie cutter from water and quickly dry before using to cut 10 hearts from chocolate. Reheat in hot water frequently to maintain smooth cutting. Remove knife from water and quickly dry before slicing neat lines in remaining chocolate to create 10 (1" × 4.5") bars. Place hearts and bars in freezer 10 minutes.

11. Remove hearts and bars from freezer and use an offset spatula or butter knife to carefully remove from baking sheet and set aside on a clean sheet of parchment paper.

12. To Assemble: On each serving plate, smear 1 tablespoon of raspberry jam across plate. Place one Chocolate Cake on top of jam. Place one bar White Chocolate Decoration against one side of Cake. Place 2 Raspberry Meringues and 1–2 dollops Raspberry Whipping Cream on or beside each cake. Finish with 3 fresh raspberries each, on top and to the sides of the Cake, and a sprinkling of edible gold leaf on top of raspberries. Press White Chocolate Decoration heart onto one dollop of Whipping Cream. Serve immediately or refrigerate in an airtight container up to 1 day.

St. Patrick's Day Irish Coffee Tarts

Sunshine Seasons, St. Patrick's Day

· · · · ✳ · · ·

Sunshine Seasons is a great place to bring the family to eat when you're spending a day at EPCOT. Several cafeteria-style counters offer a variety of cuisines, so everyone leaves happy. As an added bonus, a couple of seasonal items are almost always available, like these St. Patrick's Day Irish Coffee Tarts. Irish Crème coffee creamer can usually be found in stores around St. Patrick's Day and can be stored unopened for months at a time. Be sure to stock up so you can make these tarts well into the summer!

SERVES 2

FOR CHOCOLATE COFFEE TARTS

1⅓ cups all-purpose flour

2 tablespoons unsweetened cocoa powder

1 tablespoon instant coffee powder

¼ cup granulated sugar

¼ teaspoon salt

¾ cup salted butter, cold and cubed

1 large egg

½ teaspoon vanilla extract

FOR IRISH COFFEE CRÉMEUX

3 egg yolks

¼ cup granulated sugar

⅔ cup heavy whipping cream

1. To make Chocolate Coffee Tarts: In bowl of a food processor, add flour, cocoa powder, coffee powder, sugar, and salt and pulse 1 minute until combined. Add butter cubes one at a time while continuing to pulse until mixture is crumbly. Add egg and vanilla and pulse 1 minute more to combine.

2. Scoop dough onto a lightly floured surface and roll into a ball, and then flatten into a disk roughly ½" thick. Wrap in plastic wrap and refrigerate 1 hour.

3. Preheat oven to 350°F. Place sheets of parchment paper in two 4" tart pans and set aside.

4. Remove dough from refrigerator and let sit 10 minutes at room temperature. On a lightly floured surface, roll out dough to ¼" thickness. Using tart pans as a guide, cut 2 circles and 2 strips from dough to line insides of prepared tart pans. Poke bottoms with a fork.

(continued) ▶

½ cup whole milk

5 tablespoons Irish Crème coffee creamer

1 cup dark chocolate chips

FOR MINT MOUSSE

2 ounces cream cheese, softened

½ cup heavy whipping cream

2 tablespoons confectioners' sugar

⅛ teaspoon mint extract

½ teaspoon vanilla extract

4 drops green gel food coloring

FOR ASSEMBLY

4 teaspoons green frosting

4 (0.75") shamrock decor pieces

2 teaspoons shamrock sprinkles

5. Line insides of pans with parchment paper, fill with pie weights, and bake 18–23 minutes until crusts are dry and baked through. Remove from oven, and then remove pie weights and allow to cool completely, about 30 minutes.

6. To make Irish Coffee Crémeux: In a medium bowl, stir together egg yolks and sugar. Set aside.

7. In a small saucepan over medium heat, add cream, milk, and Irish Crème creamer and bring to a simmer, 2–4 minutes. Remove from heat and allow to cool 2 minutes.

8. While whisking continuously, pour milk mixture in a stream into yolk mixture, being careful not to allow egg yolks to cook. Whisk 3–5 minutes until custard has thickened.

9. Pour chocolate chips into a large bowl and pour hot custard over chocolate. Let sit 5 minutes. Whisk to melt chocolate and combine. Cover and set aside in refrigerator.

10. To make Mint Mousse: In bowl of a stand mixer fitted with whisk attachment, add cream cheese and whip until fluffy, 3–5 minutes. Add in cream, sugar, mint and vanilla extracts, and green coloring and whip until stiff peaks form, 4–6 minutes. Scoop into a piping bag fitted with a flat tip and set aside.

11. To Assemble: Scoop Irish Coffee Crémeux into Chocolate Coffee Tart shells (excess Crémeux can be eaten or discarded) and smooth tops. Pipe a ribbon of Mint Mousse onto each top. Squirt 2 dollops of green frosting on each Tart and place one shamrock decor piece on each dollop. Top ribbon with shamrock sprinkles and serve immediately.

Serving Tip

Disney makes adorable and delicious shamrock decor for these tarts, but they might be difficult to replicate at home. Instead, check the cake decoration section of your local grocery store for sugar shamrocks to use instead.

Fourth of July Liege Waffle

Connections Café, Fourth of July

· · · ✦ · · ·

This treat dresses the beloved waffle up in red, white, and blue for America's birthday! Disney has been making lots of Liege waffle varieties in recent years; some of the kinds they sell regularly or seasonally are chocolate, powdered sugar, Orange Bird (made with orange-flavored batter), and Valentine's Day (decorated with hearts). Which one will you be grabbing next time you're at EPCOT?

MAKES 6–8 WAFFLES

½ cup warm whole milk, 110°F

1 teaspoon fast-rising instant yeast

2 cups all-purpose flour

1 large egg

3 tablespoons light brown sugar

1 teaspoon vanilla extract

¼ teaspoon salt

10 tablespoons salted butter, melted

½ cup pearl sugar

1 cup vanilla melting wafers

2 drops blue gel food coloring

1 teaspoon white pearl sprinkles

½ cup white vanilla frosting

6 tablespoons red, white, and blue sprinkles

1. In a medium bowl, pour warm milk and then sprinkle yeast on top of milk. Allow to bloom 5 minutes. Add in flour, egg, brown sugar, vanilla, salt, and melted butter. Stir until combined. Cover with a clean towel and set in a warm place to rise 1 hour.

2. Once dough rises, fold in pearl sugar.

3. Place vanilla melting wafers in a small microwave-safe bowl, microwave on half power 30 seconds, and stir. Repeat until wafers are melted. Stir in blue food coloring.

4. Line a half-sized baking sheet with parchment paper and spread blue vanilla mixture in a thin (2mm) layer over parchment paper. While still wet, use a small Mickey cookie cutter to make 6–8 Mickeys. Top each Mickey with a few white pearl sprinkles. Refrigerate baking sheet to set, about 45 minutes.

5. Once set, carefully separate Mickeys from the parchment paper and set aside.

(continued) ▶

6. Preheat Belgian waffle iron to medium-high heat. Grease with nonstick cooking spray. Use a 3-tablespoon cookie scoop to scoop up some batter. Place batter ball on center of waffle iron and use a greased spatula to slightly flatten it. Shut waffle iron and cook 2–2½ minutes until waffle is golden brown and cooked through. Remove from iron to a large plate and repeat with remaining batter. Allow waffles to cool completely, at least 30 minutes.

7. Use an offset spatula or dinner knife to spread a thin layer of white vanilla frosting around outer edges of each waffle. Top with red, white, and blue sprinkles immediately, while white frosting is still wet. Add a small dab of white vanilla frosting to center of each waffle and place one blue vanilla Mickey on white frosting dab. Allow white frosting to harden slightly, about 30 minutes, then serve. Leftovers may be stored in an airtight container at room temperature up to 3 days.

See Turkey Poutine recipe on next page ▶

Turkey Poutine

Refreshment Port, Thanksgiving

· · · · ✳ · · ·

A typical poutine includes French fries, gravy, and cheese curds, but Refreshment Port, located close to the Canada pavilion, wanted to kick it up a notch and include elements from a classic Thanksgiving feast! Canadians celebrate Thanksgiving just like Americans do, but instead of the fourth Thursday of November, Canucks celebrate on the second Monday in October. Whether you make this poutine in October, November, or even July is up to you!

SERVES 6

FOR CRANBERRY RELISH

12 ounces fresh cranberries

1 medium orange, peel on and sliced

1 cup granulated sugar

FOR ASSEMBLY

6 cups cooked frozen French fries

1½ cups turkey gravy

1½ cups shredded cooked turkey

1½ cups crispy fried onions

1. To make Cranberry Relish: Place cranberries, orange slices, and sugar in bowl of a food processor and blend until smooth. Pour into a medium bowl, cover, and refrigerate at least 1 hour up to overnight.

2. To Assemble: Place 1 cup hot French fries on each of six serving plates and drizzle with turkey gravy, then pile on Cranberry Relish, shredded turkey, and crispy fried onions. Serve immediately.

Serving Tip

If you want to serve this for a party or with leftovers the day after Thanksgiving, simply place all the fixings in separate bowls on a serving table for guests to assemble.

Chocolate Peppermint Shake

Holiday Sweets & Treats, Christmas

· · · ✦ · · ·

The full name of this treat is "Chocolate Peppermint Shake Featuring Twinings®
Peppermint Cheer Tea." Twinings is a popular British brand of tea products that began
all the way back in 1706. Served during the holiday season, this shake
will transport your taste buds to a lovely Christmas in England. Although
EPCOT uses Twinings tea to make their Chocolate Peppermint Shake,
you can use any peppermint tea you like.

SERVES 1

¼ cup boiling water
2 peppermint tea bags
3 cups chocolate ice
  cream

1. Pour boiling water into a mug and add tea bags. Allow to
   steep 5 minutes, remove tea bags, and refrigerate mug to
   chill completely, about 1 hour.

2. Once tea is chilled, add to a blender and add in chocolate
   ice cream. Blend until combined and creamy. Pour into
   a small plastic or glass cup and serve immediately with
   a straw.

Disney Parks Tip

*You may be tempted to walk right through the United King-
dom pavilion at EPCOT since they don't have a ride, but
right behind the Twinings shop (The Tea Caddy) is a fun
hedge maze with very few crowds that is a great place to
play. Check it out next time you're in EPCOT!*

Maple Bûche de Noël

Holiday Hearth Desserts, Christmas

· · · ✴ · · ·

This version of the classic log-shaped treat has a gingerbread-flavored cake with maple and cranberry inside. It's a stunning dessert that guests may start requesting every holiday season. Holiday Hearth Desserts is in the Odyssey pavilion, which you can find between the Test Track attraction and the Mexico pavilion in EPCOT. It is a mixed-use site that houses lots of fun venues, and the Holiday Hearth treat stand is one that you shouldn't miss!

MAKES 3 CAKES

FOR GINGERBREAD CAKE

3 large eggs, separated
¼ cup granulated sugar
¼ cup molasses
¼ cup honey
1 tablespoon salted butter, softened
1 cup all-purpose flour
½ teaspoon baking soda
½ teaspoon ground ginger
½ teaspoon ground cinnamon
½ teaspoon salt

FOR MAPLE FILLING

1½ cups heavy whipping cream
⅓ cup confectioners' sugar
1 teaspoon maple flavoring

1. To make Gingerbread Cake: Preheat oven to 375°F. Grease a 15" × 10" jellyroll pan with nonstick cooking spray, then line with parchment paper. Grease parchment paper with nonstick cooking spray and set aside.

2. In bowl of a stand mixer fitted with whisk attachment, add egg whites and whip on high speed until soft peaks form, about 3 minutes. Add in sugar and continue to whip until stiff peaks form, about another 3 minutes. Scoop into a medium bowl and set aside. Wipe out bowl of stand mixer.

3. In clean stand mixer bowl fitted with whisk attachment, add egg yolks and whip on high speed about 3 minutes or until creamy. Add in molasses, honey, and butter and whisk an additional 1 minute. Add in flour, baking soda, ginger, cinnamon, and salt, and whisk 2 more minutes to combine.

4. Remove bowl from stand mixer and gently fold egg white mixture into batter. Once fully incorporated, pour into prepared pan and smooth across pan. Bake 11–15 minutes until a knife inserted comes out clean. Allow to cool completely in pan, about 45 minutes.

(continued) ▶

FOR MERINGUE MUSHROOMS

3 large egg whites

3 tablespoons granulated sugar

¹⁄₈ teaspoon cream of tartar

¹⁄₄ teaspoon vanilla extract

¹⁄₈ teaspoon salt

FOR ASSEMBLY

¹⁄₂ cup plus 1 tablespoon confectioners' sugar

¹⁄₂ cup cranberry sauce

1 cup chocolate frosting

1 cup canned whipped cream

6 holly sugar decorations

1 tablespoon holiday sprinkles

5. To make Maple Filling: In clean bowl of a stand mixer fitted with whisk attachment, add in heavy cream, sugar, and maple flavoring and whisk on high speed until stiff peaks form, about 5 minutes.

6. To make Meringue Mushrooms: Preheat oven to 225°F. Line a half-sized baking sheet with parchment paper and set aside.

7. In the top bowl of a double boiler over medium heat, add egg whites and sugar. Whisk until mixture reaches 110°F on a candy thermometer and remove from heat. Scoop into bowl of a stand mixer fitted with whisk attachment and whisk on low while adding cream of tartar, vanilla, and salt. Raise speed to high and whip until very stiff peaks form, about 3 minutes. Scoop into a piping bag fitted with a small round tip and pipe upright mushroom shapes onto prepared baking sheet, using all the meringue. Bake in preheated oven about 2 hours or until Mushrooms are very dry. Turn off oven but leave pan inside overnight to cool completely. Carefully remove Mushrooms from pan and set aside.

8. To Assemble: Once Gingerbread Cake is completely cooled, invert onto a large kitchen towel that has been sprinkled with ¹⁄₂ cup confectioners' sugar. Spread Maple Filling across entire Cake surface. Measure about 2" from one of the short ends of the Cake and spread a line of cranberry sauce across short side. Gently roll Cake into a log shape, starting on short side with cranberry sauce.

9. Frost entire top surface with chocolate frosting. Use a fork to scrape a wood-like texture into chocolate frosting. Cut log in half to make 2 shorter logs. Top each with squirts of whipped cream and place candy holly and Meringue Mushrooms on top. Finish with holiday sprinkles and a dusting of remaining confectioners' sugar and serve. Leftovers can be refrigerated in an airtight container up to 2 days.

Pastrami on Rye

L'Chaim! Holiday Kitchen, Hanukkah

· · · ✳ · · ·

Observant Jews don't eat pork products, and while not all deli meats are considered kosher (in compliance with Orthodox Jewish diet standards) friendly, kosher pastrami is a beef product that is especially popular at Jewish delis. This sandwich is as simple as it is delicious and can be enjoyed all year long, not just at Hanukkah! If you can't find prepackaged pastrami at the grocery store, check the deli counter to see if they have any fresh sliced.

SERVES 2

2 slices swirled rye bread

2 tablespoons deli mustard

4 ounces thin-sliced pastrami

1 kosher pickle spear, halved

1. Place rye bread slices on a plate or cutting board and spread 1 tablespoon mustard on each slice.

2. Pile pastrami onto mustard side of one slice of bread and top with remaining rye slice. Cut sandwich diagonally in half. Place one pickle half on each half sandwich. Drive a wooden toothpick through each pickle spear and sandwich. Place on two plates and serve immediately.

Smoked Salmon Potato Latkes

L'Chaim! Holiday Kitchen, Hanukkah

. . . ✦ . . .

Many families choose to include latkes every year in their Hanukkah celebrations, as they are delicious and have a strong connection to the Jewish faith. In the story of the Maccabees, the Temple in Jerusalem only had enough oil to keep the menorah lit for one day—but miraculously the menorah burned brightly for eight days. Therefore, many fried foods (including latkes) are consumed around Hanukkah to give thanks for the miracle of the oil.

MAKES 6 LATKES

½ cup vegetable oil, for frying

2 large russet potatoes, peeled

1 small yellow onion, peeled

1 large egg

1 tablespoon all-purpose flour

½ teaspoon salt

¼ teaspoon ground black pepper

1 (4-ounce) package smoked salmon

2 tablespoons diced red onion

1 tablespoon capers

½ cup sour cream

1 tablespoon fresh diced dill

6 small sprigs fresh parsley

1. Pour oil into a deep frying pan or Dutch oven over medium heat and allow to come to 350°F.

2. Using a food processor or hand grater, grate potatoes and yellow onion. Place in a paper towel–lined bowl and allow to release liquid 10 minutes, then squeeze dry with fresh paper towels. Place in a clean medium bowl and add egg, flour, salt, and pepper. Stir well to combine.

3. Scoop out 2-tablespoon portions of potato mix and flatten in hands to form a disk. Place directly into hot oil and fry 2–3 minutes per side until browned and crispy. Remove to a paper towel–lined plate and repeat with remaining potato mix to make six latkes.

4. Chop smoked salmon into fine pieces and mix with red onion and capers in a medium bowl. Mix sour cream and fresh dill together in a small bowl. Scoop smoked salmon onto each latke, drizzle with dill sour cream, and top with a sprig of parsley. Serve immediately.

Sufganiyot

L'Chaim! Holiday Kitchen, Hanukkah

· · · ✳ · · ·

Translated from Hebrew, *sufganiyah* (plural, *sufganiyot*) means "spongy dough." These spongy little doughnuts are delightful inside and out. Filled with tart raspberry jam and covered in sweet glaze, they will be hard to keep stocked on your Hanukkah table. Just like potato latkes, sufganiyot celebrate the miracle of oil with their deep-fried preparation.

MAKES 20 MINI SUFGANIYOT

¾ **cup warm whole milk (110°F)**

1 **(0.25-ounce) packet active dry yeast**

3 **tablespoons granulated sugar**

3½ **cups all-purpose flour**

1 **teaspoon salt**

3 **large eggs**

2 **teaspoons vanilla extract, divided**

4 **tablespoons salted butter, softened**

48 **ounces vegetable oil, for frying**

2 **cups confectioners' sugar**

⅓ **cup heavy whipping cream**

1 **cup raspberry jam**

1. Pour warm milk into a small bowl and stir yeast into milk. Allow to sit 10 minutes.

2. In bowl of a stand mixer fitted with paddle attachment, add sugar, flour, and salt and stir until combined. Switch to a dough hook and add yeast mixture, eggs, and 1 teaspoon vanilla and knead 2 minutes until combined. Add in butter 1 tablespoon at a time and allow each tablespoon to incorporate. Knead 5–10 minutes until dough is springy and elastic.

3. Grease a large bowl with nonstick cooking spray. Place dough in bowl and allow to rise in a warm place until doubled, about 1 hour.

4. Dust a flat work surface with flour and turn out risen dough onto flour. Gently roll dough out to ½" thickness. Use a 2" round cutter to cut 20 circles out of the dough, and place circles on a half-sized baking sheet in a single layer. Allow to rise again in a warm place about 30 minutes or until puffy.

5. Preheat oil in a large pot over medium heat to 350°F. Gently slide 4–5 circles at a time into hot oil to fry, careful not to overcrowd pan. Fry 1–2 minutes per side until golden brown and cooked through. Remove to a paper towel–lined baking sheet and repeat until all circles are fried. Allow to cool 30 minutes.

6. In a medium bowl, mix sugar, cream, and remaining 1 teaspoon vanilla to make a glaze. Set aside.

7. Scoop raspberry jam into a piping bag fitted with a small round tip. Press round tip into side of a cooled dough ball and squirt about 1 teaspoon of jam into ball. Repeat with remaining balls. Drizzle with prepared glaze and serve immediately.

Disney Parks Tip

During the Festival of the Holidays at EPCOT, a Hanukkah storyteller between the France and Moroccan pavilions recounts holiday traditions around the world with music and props. It is fun and informative!

Black and White Cookies

L'Chaim! Holiday Kitchen, Hanukkah

· · · · ✳ · · ·

The Jewish community is an integral part of New York City culture, as are black and white cookies. The black and white colors of the cookie are sometimes seen as representing the light and dark themes of traditional Hanukkah stories. During the Festival of the Holidays at EPCOT, there is a Holiday Cookie Stroll where you receive a stamp in your festival passport at each location you order an eligible cookie. Once you've scored five stamps, you get a special sweet treat and a small prize too. The Black and White Cookie is part of the Holiday Cookie Stroll, but eating it is a prize in and of itself!

MAKES 9 COOKIES

FOR COOKIES
1/3 cup salted butter, softened
1/2 cup granulated sugar
1 large egg
1 1/4 cups all-purpose flour
1/2 teaspoon baking powder
1/2 teaspoon salt
1/2 teaspoon vanilla extract
1/2 teaspoon lemon extract
1/3 cup whole milk

1. To make Cookies: Preheat oven to 375°F. Line a full-sized baking sheet with parchment paper and set aside.

2. In bowl of a stand mixer fitted with paddle attachment, cream together butter and sugar on medium speed 2 minutes. Add in egg and mix 1 minute more.

3. While mixer is running on low speed, add flour, baking powder, and salt and mix 1 minute to combine. Add vanilla and lemon extracts and mix 1 minute more. Lastly, drizzle in milk and mix 1 minute more.

4. Use a 3-tablespoon cookie scoop to scoop out 9 dough balls onto prepared baking sheet. Bake 12–15 minutes until a knife inserted in center comes out clean. Remove from oven and allow to cool on pan completely, about 45 minutes.

(continued) ▶

FOR GLAZES

2½ cups confectioners' sugar

4 tablespoons whole milk, divided

¼ teaspoon vanilla extract

¼ cup unsweetened cocoa powder

5. To make Glazes: In a medium bowl, combine confectioners' sugar and 3 tablespoons milk and whisk until no more powder remains. Pour ½ mixture into a second medium bowl. In one bowl, add vanilla extract and stir to combine. In second bowl, add cocoa powder and remaining 1 tablespoon milk. Stir to combine until smooth.

6. Once Cookies are completely cooled, place on a wire rack over a full-sized baking sheet. Use a spoon to carefully glaze one half of the top of each Cookie in vanilla Glaze and let dry about 10 minutes. Then glaze the other half with chocolate Glaze and allow to dry another 10 minutes. Serve. Leftover Cookies can be refrigerated in an airtight container up to 5 days.

Chicken and Matzo Ball Soup

L'Chaim! Holiday Kitchen, Hanukkah

· · · ✳ · · ·

Although chicken and matzo ball soup is served during the Festival of the Holidays in November and December at EPCOT, matzo ball soup is more typically served in Jewish tradition as part of the Passover meal. This is because when the Israelites fled Egypt, they could only carry unleavened bread, or matzo, which is what matzo balls are made from. Those of the Jewish faith eat matzo to remember that event.

SERVES 6

FOR MATZO BALLS

2 large eggs

2 tablespoons vegetable oil

½ cup matzo ball mix

FOR SOUP

1 tablespoon vegetable oil

6 large carrots, peeled and chopped

1 medium yellow onion, peeled and diced

3 teaspoons minced garlic

2 boneless skinless chicken thighs, cubed

48 ounces chicken broth

1 teaspoon salt

¼ teaspoon ground black pepper

1 teaspoon dried dill

2 dried bay leaves

1. To make Matzo Balls: In a medium bowl, beat eggs and oil together. Add in matzo ball mix and stir to combine. Refrigerate 20 minutes.

2. To make Soup: In a medium pot or Dutch oven, heat oil 2 minutes over medium heat. Add in carrots and onion and stir until softened, about 5 minutes. Add garlic and cook 2 minutes more.

3. Add in chicken, broth, salt, pepper, dill, and bay leaves. Bring to a boil, then reduce heat to low, cover, and simmer 20 minutes.

4. Remove matzo mixture from refrigerator. Use a 1–2 tablespoon cookie scoop to make balls with dough, and then tighten balls with wet hands. Place on a large plate and refrigerate until ready to use.

5. Once Soup has simmered 20 minutes, add in Matzo Balls, then keep simmering Soup, covered, 20 more minutes.

6. Remove bay leaves and ladle soup into six serving bowls. Serve immediately. Leftovers can be refrigerated in an airtight container up to 3 days and reheated in a pot on the stove or in the microwave.

Potato Knish

L'Chaim! Holiday Kitchen, Hanukkah

· · · ✳ · · ·

The potato knish originated in Jewish communities of Eastern Europe and was brought to the United States by immigrants to New York City. Popular from the start for being low cost and filling, the knish is still popular to this day for its tastiness and versatility. Many Jewish families have a tradition of making knishes during Hanukkah. Some knishes are even sweet, with a fruit jam filling! However you like your knish, you can now make these delectable "pillows of filling" at home.

MAKES 24 KNISHES

FOR DOUGH

$3\frac{1}{4}$ cups all-purpose flour

1 teaspoon salt

$\frac{3}{4}$ cup cold salted butter, cubed

$\frac{3}{4}$ cup sour cream

2 tablespoons water

FOR FILLING

2 large russet potatoes, peeled and cubed

$\frac{1}{4}$ cup salted butter

1 large yellow onion, peeled and diced

$\frac{1}{2}$ teaspoon salt

$\frac{1}{4}$ teaspoon ground black pepper

4 large eggs, divided

1. To make Dough: In a food processor, add flour and salt and pulse several times to mix. While continuing to pulse, add in butter one cube at a time until all is added. Dough will be dry and crumbly. Add in sour cream and water until Dough comes together.

2. Remove Dough from food processor, cut in half, and flatten into 2 disks. Wrap in plastic wrap and refrigerate 2 hours up to overnight.

3. To make Filling: Fill a medium pot with water and bring to a boil over medium-high heat. Add in potato cubes and boil until soft, 10–15 minutes. Potatoes are ready when they break easily with a fork. Drain water and place potatoes in a large bowl. Set aside.

4. In a large skillet over medium heat, add butter and onion and stir until onion is soft, 8–10 minutes. Add cooked onion to potatoes and stir and mash until smooth. Season with salt and pepper and refrigerate 30 minutes.

1 cup sour cream

**2 teaspoons fresh
  chopped dill**

1 teaspoon lemon juice

5. Add 3 eggs to chilled potato mixture and stir to combine. Set aside.

6. Preheat oven to 400°F and line a full-sized baking sheet with parchment paper.

7. Roll out each Dough disk to $1/8$" thickness. Cut into 24 squares, approximately 4" × 4" each. Scoop 1 tablespoon of Filling into center of each Dough square and close by bringing opposite corners together and pinching along the edges to create a seal. Flip sealed side over and place knishes flat side up on prepared baking sheet.

8. Beat remaining egg in a small bowl and brush over tops of knishes. Bake 15–20 minutes until Dough is golden brown. Remove from oven and let cool 15 minutes.

9. To make Herb Sour Cream: Mix sour cream, dill, and lemon juice in a small bowl. Drizzle over top of slightly cooled knishes. Serve immediately.

Egg Cream

L'Chaim! Holiday Kitchen, Hanukkah

· · · ✳ · · ·

"Egg cream" is a bit of a misnomer since this drink contains no egg and no cream. But the name is derived from the Yiddish *echt keem*, which means "pure sweetness," and it got lost in translation along the way. While egg creams are getting harder to find in New York City or other Jewish communities, EPCOT serves them up to keep the tradition alive. Many Jewish families make them at home during Hanukkah; they are super simple to make and use only three ingredients that you probably already have on hand!

SERVES 1

3 tablespoons chocolate syrup
¼ cup whole milk
¾ cup club soda

In a 16-ounce plastic or glass cup, add in chocolate syrup and milk and stir to combine. Add club soda and stir quickly to create a froth. Serve immediately.

Cooking Hack

A traditional egg cream uses Fox's U-Bet Chocolate Flavored Syrup due to its bittersweet chocolate flavor and thin consistency to better mix into the drink. Try using Fox's U-Bet when you make an egg cream at home!

CHAPTER 6

Disney's Hollywood Studios & Disney's Animal Kingdom

This chapter takes you on a delicious journey through two iconic parks: Disney's Hollywood Studios and Disney's Animal Kingdom! While Animal Kingdom is famously known for its exotic adventures, only one of its festive treats, offered during the Christmas season, is included in this book: the toasty S'mores Hot Cocoa from Isle of Java. Disney seems to focus most of their holiday spirit on the other Parks, but you can enjoy this holiday treat, as well as decorations focusing on nature's view of wintertime. For instance, an interactive "show" called Merry Menagerie can be seen in front of the Tree of Life: puppeteers animating cute penguins, foxes, and polar bears that you can pet and play with!

And thanks to Disney's Hollywood Studios, you can enjoy a whole cast of flavors inspired by holidays throughout the seasons! Valentine's Day, Black History Month/Celebrate Soulfully, Mardi Gras, May the Fourth, Pride Month, the Fourth of July, Halloween, and Christmas are all celebrated in the Park with mouthwatering bites and satisfying beverages that you can now make in your own kitchen. Dive into iconic fare like the vibrant Strawberry Red Velvet Whoopie Pies from The Trolley Car Café for Valentine's Day or indulge in the decadent Tiana's Mardi Gras Milkshake from Hollywood Scoops!

STAR WARS:
GALAXY'S EDGE

1 7
6 9

AN INCREDIBLE
CELEBRATION

11

5
13
14
4

COMMISSARY LANE

12

ECHO LAKE

2

HOLLYWOOD BOULEVARD

ENTRANCE

DISNEY'S HOLLYWOOD STUDIOS

1. **SWEET POTATO LUNCH BOX TARTS**
   (Woody's Lunch Box, Black History Month/Celebrate Soulfully)

2. **STRAWBERRY RED VELVET WHOOPIE PIES**
   (The Trolley Car Café, Valentine's Day)

3. **TIANA'S MARDI GRAS MILKSHAKES**
   (Hollywood Scoops, Mardi Gras)

4. **INTERSTELLAR SWEET AND CRUNCHY POPCORN**
   (Popcorn Stands, May the Fourth)

5. **JETTISON JUICE**
   (ABC Commissary, May the Fourth)

6. **PRIDE LUNCH BOX TARTS**
   (Woody's Lunch Box, Pride Month)

7. **LUNCH BOX PARFAITS**
   (Woody's Lunch Box, Fourth of July)

8. **CANDY CORN MILKSHAKE**
   (Hollywood Scoops, Halloween)

9. **PUMPKIN LUNCH BOX TARTS**
   (Woody's Lunch Box, Halloween)

10. **PUMPKIN PATCH COOKIES**
    (Catalina Eddie's, Halloween)

11. **FROZEN SALTED CARAMEL HOT CHOCOLATE**
    (PizzeRizzo, Christmas)

12. **HOLIDAY TREE MARSHMALLOWS**
    (Dockside Diner, Christmas)

13. **HOLIDAY MINNIE MOUSE BUNDT CAKES**
    (ABC Commissary, Christmas)

14. **REINDEER MOUSSE**
    (ABC Commissary, Christmas)

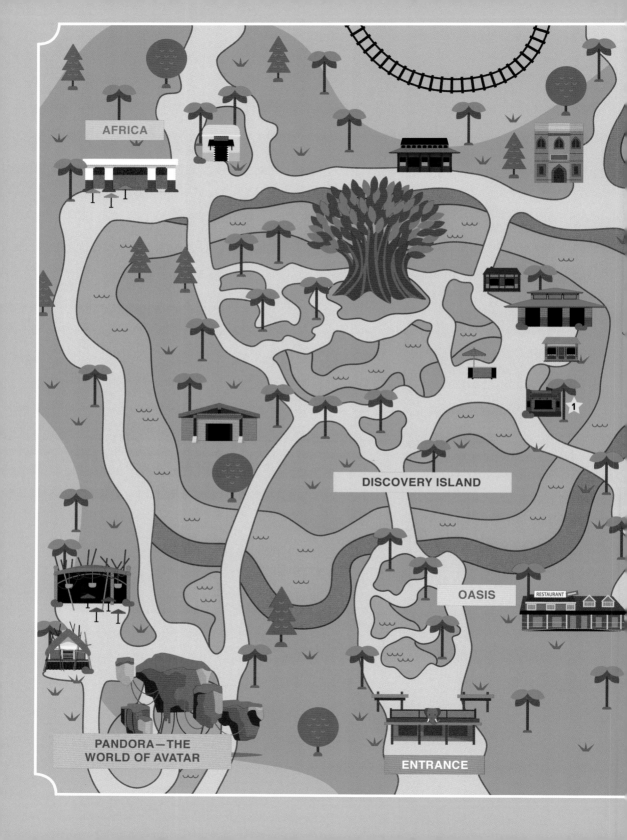

ASIA

DINOLAND U.S.A.

DISNEY'S
ANIMAL KINGDOM

1 **S'MORES HOT COCOA**
(Isle of Java, Christmas)

Sweet Potato Lunch Box Tarts

**Woody's Lunch Box, Disney's Hollywood Studios,
Black History Month/Celebrate Soulfully**

· · · ✳ · · ·

Sweet potatoes are not only delicious; they also play a key role in the
Black community of the United States. Cultivated by African slaves on American soil,
they are a hearty, nutritious crop that became a mainstay of the diet of
enslaved African Americans. Because of this, sweet potatoes have become
prominent in southern dishes both sweet and savory. Sweet potato pie is
now a staple across southern households, and while it's usually served
at Thanksgiving, it can be enjoyed at any occasion.

SERVES 4

FOR PASTRIES

1 (2-count) box
refrigerated pie crusts

1 cup canned yams,
drained

1 tablespoon salted
butter, melted

2 tablespoons light
brown sugar

2 teaspoons granulated
sugar

1/4 teaspoon ground
cinnamon

1/8 teaspoon ground
nutmeg

1/2 teaspoon vanilla
extract

1. To make Pastries: Preheat oven to 450°F and line a half-sized baking sheet with parchment paper.

2. Remove pie crusts from refrigerator, let sit 45 minutes, then unroll onto parchment paper. Fold each circular crust in half and use a sharp knife to cut 2 double-thick rectangles (about 3" × 2.5") to make 8 total rectangles. Discard excess crust pieces and lay out rectangles on parchment paper. Set aside.

3. In a medium mixing bowl, add yams, butter, brown sugar, granulated sugar, cinnamon, nutmeg, and vanilla. Use a potato masher or whisk to smash into a uniform smooth consistency. Scoop 2 tablespoons of mash down center of 4 pie crust rectangles, keeping edges clean (eat or discard excess filling if any). Run a wet finger along clean crust edges. Use your fingers to gently stretch remaining 4 rectangles of crust to accommodate filling and place on top

FOR CINNAMON–BROWN
SUGAR ICING

$\frac{1}{2}$ **cup salted butter,
softened**

$\frac{1}{4}$ **cup light brown sugar**

**2 cups confectioners'
sugar**

$\frac{1}{2}$ **teaspoon vanilla
extract**

1 teaspoon whole milk

$\frac{1}{2}$ **teaspoon ground
cinnamon**

FOR ASSEMBLY

**4 tablespoons chopped
pecans**

12 mini marshmallows

of filling. Press gently on edges to adhere top and bottom
to one another, then use a fork to crimp around sides of all
4 Pastries. Use fork to gently poke top of each Pastry once.

4. Bake 14–16 minutes until golden brown. Remove from oven
and allow to cool on pan completely, about 45 minutes.

5. To make Cinnamon–Brown Sugar Icing: In bowl of a
stand mixer fitted with whisk attachment, add butter and
brown sugar and mix 3 minutes until creamy. Add in
confectioners' sugar, vanilla, milk, and cinnamon, mixing
after each addition 30 seconds.

6. To Assemble: Spread Cinnamon–Brown Sugar Icing on
top of each Pastry, then sprinkle each with 1 tablespoon
chopped pecans and 3 mini marshmallows. Use a kitchen
torch to lightly toast marshmallows. Serve immediately or
refrigerate in an airtight container up to 3 days.

Strawberry Red Velvet Whoopie Pies

The Trolley Car Café, Disney's Hollywood Studios, Valentine's Day

· · · ✦ · · ·

Whoopie pies are basically flat cupcakes with frosting in the middle instead of on top. In fact, if you'd rather make these Strawberry Red Velvet Whoopie Pies as cupcakes instead, you totally can! Simply bake the batter in a cupcake tin, then hollow out the middle of the cooled cupcakes, pipe in the Cream Cheese Buttercream, and swirl Strawberry Buttercream on top! The Trolley Car Café is also a Starbucks location at Disney's Hollywood Studios, so grab a Strawberry Crème Frappuccino to go along with your red velvet treat and enjoy your Valentine's Day.

MAKES 12 WHOOPIE PIES

FOR RED VELVET CAKE

1 (15.25-ounce) box red velvet cake mix

1¼ cups room-temperature water

½ cup vegetable oil

3 large eggs

FOR CREAM CHEESE BUTTERCREAM

8 ounces cream cheese, softened

½ cup salted butter, softened

4 cups confectioners' sugar

2 teaspoons vanilla extract

3 drops red gel food coloring

1. To make Red Velvet Cake: Preheat oven to 350°F. Spray two twelve-divot whoopie pie pans with nonstick cooking spray and set aside.

2. In a large bowl, combine cake mix, water, vegetable oil, and eggs. Divide into pan divots and bake 10–15 minutes until a toothpick inserted in center comes out clean. Remove from oven and allow to cool in pan 10 minutes, and then cool completely on a wire rack 1 hour.

3. To make Cream Cheese Buttercream: In bowl of a stand mixer fitted with whisk attachment, add softened cream cheese and butter and whisk 2 minutes or until smooth. Add in sugar, vanilla, and red food coloring, and whisk 2 minutes more. Scoop into a piping bag fitted with a large star tip and set aside.

(continued) ▶

**1 cup salted butter,
softened**

**4 cups confectioners'
sugar**

¼ cup strawberry purée

FOR ASSEMBLY

**1 cup assorted Valentine
sprinkles**

**6 whole fresh
strawberries, halved**

4. To make Strawberry Buttercream: In clean bowl of a stand mixer fitted with whisk attachment, add softened butter and whisk 2 minutes or until smooth. Add in sugar and strawberry purée and whisk 2 minutes more. Scoop into a piping bag fitted with a large star tip and set aside.

5. To Assemble: Place one Red Velvet Cake round on a plate flat side up. Pipe a swirl of Cream Cheese Buttercream on Cake. Press 1 tablespoon sprinkles onto Cream Cheese Buttercream, pressing all around sides. Top with second Cake, flat side down. Set on plate and pipe a swirl of Strawberry Buttercream on top. Press a strawberry half onto Strawberry Buttercream. Repeat with remaining Cake and Buttercreams. Serve immediately or refrigerate in an airtight container up to 3 days.

Tiana's Mardi Gras Milkshakes

Hollywood Scoops, Disney's Hollywood Studios, Mardi Gras

. . . ✦ . . .

Get out your trumpets and cue the drums, because here comes the tastiest milkshake your Mardi Gras parties have ever seen. Have you ever tucked into a doughnut and wished you had a refreshing milkshake to go with it? This treat is for you! A convenient drink and dessert all in one, you'll still have a hand free to hold your parade parasol. Take a closer look for another fun detail: Each of the sprinkle colors has a different texture. Of course, at home you can use any sprinkles you like, but the variation does add a certain je ne sais quoi!

SERVES 6

1 large egg
$1/2$ cup buttermilk
$1/4$ cup granulated sugar
1 cup all-purpose flour
1 teaspoon baking powder
$1/4$ teaspoon salt
1 teaspoon ground cinnamon
24 tablespoons white frosting
6 teaspoons purple stick sprinkles
6 teaspoons plus 12 tablespoons gold circle sprinkles, divided
6 teaspoons green sugar sprinkles

1. Preheat oven to 325°F. Grease a six-divot doughnut pan with nonstick cooking spray and set aside.

2. In bowl of a stand mixer fitted with paddle attachment, add egg, buttermilk, and sugar and mix 2 minutes or until well combined. Add flour, baking powder, salt, and cinnamon one at a time and mix 1 minute after each addition.

3. Scoop batter into a piping bag and pipe into prepared doughnut pan. Bake 12–15 minutes until golden brown. Remove pan from oven and carefully remove doughnuts from pan to a wire rack to cool completely, about 30 minutes.

4. Once doughnuts are completely cooled, spread top of each doughnut with 2 tablespoons of white frosting and sprinkle with 1 teaspoon of each color sprinkle. Set aside.

(continued) ▶

18 cups vanilla ice cream

1½ cups whole milk

6 teaspoons ground cinnamon

1½ cups canned whipped cream

5. Prepare six 18-ounce plastic cups by smearing 2 tablespoons of white frosting around top outer inch of each cup and sprinkling with 2 tablespoons gold circle sprinkles, pressing lightly to let them stick to frosting.

6. In the pitcher of a blender, add 3 cups vanilla ice cream, ¼ cup whole milk, and 1 teaspoon ground cinnamon. Blend 2 minutes or until smooth and creamy. Pour into one prepared cup. Repeat with remaining ingredients and cups.

7. Squirt canned whipped cream in a circle around top of each Milkshake and place a doughnut on whipped cream. Finish with a large-gauge straw placed through center of doughnut. Enjoy immediately.

Interstellar Sweet and Crunchy Popcorn

Popcorn Stands, Disney's Hollywood Studios, May the Fourth

· · · ✦ · · ·

Blast off into a flavor galaxy with Interstellar Sweet and Crunchy Popcorn! This out-of-this-world treat combines sweet kettle corn, crunchy pecans (with a hint of spice), and cookies for a cosmic explosion in your mouth. It's the perfect way to satisfy your adventurous spirit and your sweet tooth all at once, while commemorating a day for Star Wars fans everywhere. Feeling interstellar inspiration? Crank up the spice, swap the pecans for another adventurous crunch, or even create your own cosmic concoction.

SERVES 6

FOR CANDIED PECANS
- 1/2 cup confectioners' sugar
- 1 teaspoon kosher salt
- 1 teaspoon cayenne pepper
- 4 teaspoons water
- 2 cups unsalted pecan halves

FOR ASSEMBLY
- 4 cups prepared kettle corn
- 10 chocolate sandwich cookies, broken into pieces

1. To make Candied Pecans: Preheat oven to 350°F. Line a full-sized baking sheet with parchment paper and set aside.

2. In a large bowl, whisk together confectioners' sugar, salt, cayenne pepper, and water until well combined. Add in pecans and fold until well coated. Pour onto prepared baking sheet and smooth into a single layer. Bake 10–12 minutes until coating hardens. Remove from oven and allow to cool completely on the baking pan, about 30 minutes. Break up chunks and set aside.

3. To Assemble: In an extra-large bowl, add kettle corn, chocolate cookie pieces, and Candied Pecans. Mix and scoop into six bowls or bags to serve. Leftovers can be stored in an airtight container at room temperature up to 4 days.

Jettison Juice

ABC Commissary, Disney's Hollywood Studios, May the Fourth

· · · ✦ · · ·

You're not going to want to jettison this juice! A refreshing blend of tart lemonade and sweet watermelon syrup, it will quench your thirst on May fourth—or any other day of the year. Many people are familiar with the play on words that turns "May the Force" into "May the Fourth," but have you heard of its sister holiday, Revenge of the Fifth? This riff on the title of the third episode of the Star Wars movie series, *Revenge of the Sith,* allows citizens of the galaxy an extra day to party and even more time to make amazing Star Wars–themed foods and drinks! This drink is also available at Backlot Express, PizzeRizzo, and Rosie's All-American Café.

SERVES 1

8 ounces prepared lemonade

1 ounce Monin Watermelon Syrup

Add lemonade and syrup to a cocktail shaker half full of ice. Shake well. Pour into a 16-ounce plastic cup and top with ice. Serve.

Pride Lunch Box Tarts

Woody's Lunch Box, Disney's Hollywood Studios, Pride Month

· · · ✦ · · ·

You may have heard about Pride Month in June, but have you ever heard of Gay Days? This is an "unofficial" event by Disney, but a very official event for the LGBTQIA+ community! Held one weekend a year, thousands of members and allies come to the Disneyland and Walt Disney World Resorts to support one another and show pride! Disney has recently started putting out merchandise, specialty snacks, and beverages to honor the event. If you can't make it to the Parks in person for Gay Days or Pride Month, make a batch of these Pride Lunch Box Tarts at home and share them with friends and family.

SERVES 4

FOR PASTRIES

1 (2-count) package refrigerated pie crusts

8 tablespoons guava jam

FOR PURPLE VANILLA FROSTING

½ cup salted butter, softened

2¼ cups confectioners' sugar

½ teaspoon vanilla extract

1 teaspoon whole milk

3 drops purple gel food coloring

1. To make Pastries: Preheat oven to 450°F and line a half-sized baking sheet with parchment paper.

2. Remove pie crusts from refrigerator and let sit 45 minutes, then unroll onto parchment paper. Fold each circular crust in half and use a sharp knife to cut 2 double-thick rectangles (about 3" × 2.5") to make 8 total rectangles. Discard excess crust pieces and lay out rectangles on parchment paper. Set aside.

3. Scoop jam down center of 4 pie crust rectangles, keeping edges clean. Run a wet finger along clean edges. Use your fingers to gently stretch remaining 4 rectangles of crust to accommodate filling and place on top of filling. Press gently on edges to adhere top and bottom to one another, then use a fork to crimp around sides of all 4 Pastries. Use fork to gently poke top of each Pastry once.

(continued) ▶

145

FOR ASSEMBLY

½ **cup white chocolate chips**

2 drops blue gel food coloring

4 rainbow sour ribbons

4 tablespoons rainbow sprinkles

4. Bake 14–16 minutes until golden brown. Remove from oven and allow to cool on pan completely, about 45 minutes.

5. To make Purple Vanilla Frosting: In bowl of a stand mixer fitted with whisk attachment, add butter and whip 3 minutes or until creamy. Gradually add in sugar, vanilla, milk, and food coloring, mixing 30 seconds between additions.

6. To Assemble: Line a half-sized baking sheet with parchment paper. Place white chocolate chips in a microwave-safe bowl and microwave in 30-second increments, stirring between each, until chips just melt. Stir in blue food coloring and scoop into a piping bag fitted with a small round tip.

7. Pipe 4 Mickey shapes (about 1" in size) onto parchment paper and allow to set in freezer until hard, about 30 minutes.

8. Once Pastries are completely cool, spread Purple Vanilla Frosting on top of each Pastry, add a rainbow sour ribbon, sprinkle with rainbow sprinkles, and top with a white chocolate Mickey. Serve immediately or refrigerate in an airtight container up to 3 days.

Lunch Box Parfaits

Woody's Lunch Box, Disney's Hollywood Studios, Fourth of July

· · · ✴ · · ·

Celebrate America's birthday with this chilled treat! Fresh fruit, fluffy whipped cream, and bouncy gelatin come together in a symphony of refreshing flavors. The Fourth of July at the Disney Parks is an electrifying experience, but be prepared for the crowds! If you're opting for a calmer celebration at home, whip up an extra batch of Lunch Box Parfaits and savor the holiday in air-conditioned comfort.

SERVES 6

2 cups boiling water, divided

1 (3-ounce) box blue gelatin

2 cups cold water, divided

1 (3-ounce) box red gelatin

3 cups whipped topping, thawed

12 fresh strawberries, hulled and quartered

1 cup fresh blueberries

1. In a large bowl, combine 1 cup boiling water and blue gelatin. Whisk until dissolved, about 2 minutes. Add in 1 cup cold water and whisk again, about 30 seconds. Pour equal amounts into six 8-ounce clear plastic cups and refrigerate to set 4 hours up to overnight. Rinse bowl.

2. In clean large bowl, combine remaining 1 cup boiling water and red gelatin. Whisk until dissolved, about 2 minutes. Add remaining 1 cup cold water and whisk again 30 seconds. Pour gently into an 8" × 8" glass pan and refrigerate to set 4 hours up to overnight.

3. Once gelatins are set, use a knife to cut red gelatin into $1/2$" cubes. Set aside.

4. Scoop about 2 tablespoons whipped topping onto blue gelatin in each cup and smooth down. Arrange 4 cubes red gelatin on whipped topping against sides of cup (eat or discard any excess red gelatin). Scoop more whipped topping into each cup until topping is flush with top of cup. Place sliced strawberries and blueberries on top of whipped topping in each cup and serve immediately or refrigerate up to 2 hours before serving.

Candy Corn Milkshake

Hollywood Scoops, Disney's Hollywood Studios, Halloween

. . . * . . .

Candy corn: Love it or hate it, it's an iconic fall treat! If you're firmly in the "Candy Corn Crew," then prepare to dive into a milkshake so deliciously "corny," it'll make your taste buds do a spooky jig. This milkshake is a celebration of all things sweet and autumnal. If you grab one at Hollywood Scoops, you can savor each sip while spooky screams echo through the air courtesy of The Twilight Zone Tower of Terror! At home you can use any kind of Halloween-themed sprinkles your heart desires, from bat and pumpkin shapes to stick sprinkles in green, purple, black, and orange.

SERVES 1

1 tablespoon vanilla frosting

1 tablespoon plus 1 teaspoon Halloween sprinkles, divided

3 cups vanilla ice cream

3 ounces whole milk

1 ounce Monin Candy Corn Syrup

1 vanilla cake doughnut

1 tablespoon vanilla icing

3 candy corns

1/2 cup canned whipped cream

1. Prepare a 16-ounce plastic or glass cup by spreading vanilla frosting around outer top 1" of cup and pressing 1 tablespoon Halloween sprinkles into frosting. Set aside.

2. In the pitcher of a blender, add ice cream, milk, and syrup. Blend until smooth, about 2 minutes. Pour into prepared cup.

3. Decorate cake doughnut with a drizzle of vanilla icing, remaining 1 teaspoon 1 teaspoon Halloween sprinkles, and candy corns. Swirl whipped cream on top of milkshake and place decorated doughnut on top of whipped cream. Place a large-gauge straw through doughnut center and enjoy immediately.

Cooking Hack

Instead of a store-bought doughnut, you can make your own vanilla cake doughnut if preferred. Simply use a boxed white cake mix and dye the batter orange for extra fun. Bake prepared mix in a doughnut pan and bake in the oven for a similar amount of time as instructed for cupcakes or until a knife inserted in doughnut comes out clean.

Pumpkin Lunch Box Tarts

Woody's Lunch Box, Disney's Hollywood Studios, Halloween

· · · ✳ · · ·

Seasonal favorites are always to be found in Lunch Box Tart form at Woody's Lunch Box! This version tastes like pumpkin pie. Next time you're having the family over for Halloween, try serving these instead of pie slices—I bet they will be a hit with the kids (and the adults too!). If you're enjoying these at Disney's Hollywood Studios, grab one before you get in line for Slinky Dog Dash. This roller coaster's popularity often causes the line to be a couple of hours long, so you'll be happy you brought a snack!

SERVES 4

FOR PASTRIES

1 (2-count) package refrigerated pie crusts

$\frac{1}{2}$ cup pumpkin purée

2 teaspoons ground cinnamon

2 teaspoons granulated sugar

FOR GREEN VANILLA FROSTING

$\frac{1}{2}$ cup salted butter, softened

$2\frac{1}{4}$ cups confectioners' sugar

$\frac{1}{2}$ teaspoon vanilla extract

1 teaspoon whole milk

3 drops green gel food coloring

1. To make Pastries: Preheat oven to 450°F and line a half-sized baking sheet with parchment paper.

2. Remove pie crusts from refrigerator and let sit 45 minutes, then unroll onto parchment paper. Fold each circular crust in half and use a sharp knife to cut 2 double-thick rectangles (about 3"× 2.5") to make 8 total rectangles. Discard excess crust pieces and lay out rectangles on parchment paper. Set aside.

3. In a small bowl, mix pumpkin purée, cinnamon, and sugar. Scoop 2 tablespoons of filling down center of 4 rectangles, keeping edges clean (eat or discard excess filling if any). Run a wet finger along clean edges. Use your fingers to gently stretch remaining 4 rectangles of crust to accommodate filling and place on top of filling. Press gently on edges to adhere top and bottom to one another, then use a fork to crimp around sides of all 4 Pastries. Use fork to gently poke top of each Pastry once.

12 candy corns

4 teaspoons assorted Halloween stick sprinkles

4. Bake 14–16 minutes until golden brown. Remove from oven and allow to cool on pan completely, about 45 minutes.

5. To make Green Vanilla Frosting: In bowl of a stand mixer fitted with whisk attachment, add butter and whip 3 minutes or until creamy. Gradually add in sugar, vanilla, milk, and food coloring, mixing 30 seconds between additions.

6. To Assemble: Once Pastries are completely cool, spread Green Vanilla Frosting on top of each Pastry, place 3 candy corns on top of Green Vanilla Frosting, and sprinkle with Halloween sprinkles. Serve immediately or refrigerate in an airtight container up to 3 days.

Pumpkin Patch Cookies

Catalina Eddie's, Disney's Hollywood Studios, Halloween

· · · ✦ · · ·

This adorable cookie will make a perfect dessert at any Halloween or autumnal party. Catalina Eddie's serves these with frosting "grass" and vines and candy pumpkins on each cookie, but you can let your imagination run wild. Browse the baking section of your local grocery store during the fall months and look for fun decorations, like sugar tombstones or candy eyeballs. Let the kids create their own spooky scenes!

MAKES 12 COOKIES

FOR COOKIES
- 1/2 cup salted butter, softened
- 1/2 cup granulated sugar
- 1/4 cup light brown sugar
- 1 large egg
- 1/2 teaspoon vanilla extract
- 1 1/2 cups all-purpose flour
- 1 teaspoon cream of tartar
- 1/2 teaspoon baking soda
- 1/2 teaspoon pumpkin pie spice
- 1/4 teaspoon salt

1. To make Cookies: Preheat oven to 375°F. Line a full-sized baking sheet with parchment paper and set aside.

2. In bowl of a stand mixer fitted with paddle attachment, cream together butter and sugars on medium speed 2 minutes or until soft. Continue to mix on low, and add in egg, vanilla extract, flour, cream of tartar, baking soda, pumpkin pie spice, and salt. Mix 2 minutes more or until combined.

3. Use a 2–3-tablespoon cookie scoop to scoop 12 mounds of dough onto prepared baking sheet. Bake 10–12 minutes until browned and cooked through. Remove from oven and allow to cool on baking sheet completely, about 30 minutes.

(continued) ▶

FOR FROSTING

1/3 cup salted butter, softened

3 cups confectioners' sugar

1 teaspoon pumpkin pie spice

3 tablespoons heavy whipping cream

FOR ASSEMBLY

12 tablespoons green piping frosting

36 candy pumpkins

4. To make Frosting: In clean bowl of a stand mixer fitted with paddle attachment, cream butter until smooth, about 2 minutes. Add sugar, pumpkin pie spice, and whipping cream until smooth and combined. Once Cookies are cooled, frost each with Frosting.

5. To Assemble: Use green frosting fitted with a grass piping tip to make "grass" patches on top of Frosting. Fit green frosting with a small round tip and pipe vines around "grass" patches. Add 3 candy pumpkins to each Cookie next to "grass" patches and vines and serve. Leftovers can be refrigerated in an airtight container up to 4 days.

Frozen Salted Caramel Hot Chocolate

PizzeRizzo, Disney's Hollywood Studios, Christmas

. . . ✦ . . .

Even in the wintertime, Florida can be sweltering. Luckily, you can enjoy the flavors of the holidays with the cool, refreshing taste of a frozen beverage with this treat. PizzeRizzo is a bit of a hidden gem at Disney's Hollywood Studios, as it is tucked back behind Star Tours and is across from Muppet Vision 3D. If you aren't near PizzeRizzo, this drink is also served at ABC Commissary, Backlot Express, and Rosie's All-American Café. At home, you can sip this rich chocolate beverage whenever you want to get into the Christmas spirit.

SERVES 1

6 ounces prepared milk chocolate hot chocolate

2 ounces salted caramel syrup

3 cups crushed ice

¼ cup mini marshmallows

1 tablespoon chocolate syrup

1. Refrigerate hot chocolate until completely cooled, about 1 hour.

2. Pour chilled hot chocolate into the pitcher of a blender. Add salted caramel syrup and crushed ice and blend until smooth, about 2 minutes.

3. Pour into a 16-ounce plastic or glass cup and pile mini marshmallows on top. Drizzle marshmallows with chocolate syrup. Serve immediately with a large-gauge straw.

Disney Parks Tip

If you are feeling hot or tired on a day at the Park, head to Muppet Vision 3D, which usually doesn't have a crowd. Simply sit in the back row of the theater and ask the Cast Member on duty if you can stay for a few shows. It is the perfect place to have a little break.

Holiday Tree Marshmallows

Dockside Diner, Disney's Hollywood Studios, Christmas

· · · · ✦ · · ·

This dessert is the gift that keeps on giving. A cookie topped with jam topped with marshmallow topped with white chocolate topped with sprinkles topped with a sugar star! Dockside Diner is a great place to sit outside at Disney's Hollywood Studios during the holidays and listen to the Christmas tunes playing—and perhaps even catch sight of a few Disney characters wandering around in their festive finest.
Grab a friend or two to share one of these trees!

MAKES 12 TREES

FOR COOKIES
- 1 cup salted butter, softened
- $\frac{1}{2}$ cup plus 2 tablespoons granulated sugar, divided
- 1 teaspoon vanilla extract
- 2 cups all-purpose flour

FOR MARSHMALLOW
- $1\frac{1}{2}$ cups granulated sugar
- $\frac{2}{3}$ cup cold water
- 2 tablespoons gelatin powder
- $\frac{1}{4}$ cup hot water
- 2 teaspoons vanilla extract

1. To make Cookies: Preheat oven to 350°F. Line a half-sized baking sheet with parchment paper and set aside.

2. In bowl of a stand mixer fitted with paddle attachment, cream together butter and $\frac{1}{2}$ cup sugar, then add vanilla and flour. Mix until dough is coming together and not crumbly, about 2 minutes.

3. Sprinkle 1 tablespoon sugar across a flat surface and place dough on sugar. Sprinkle top of dough with remaining 1 tablespoon sugar and roll out dough to $\frac{1}{4}$" thickness. Use a biscuit cutter or cookie cutter to cut out 12 (3") circles. Carefully transfer dough circles onto prepared baking sheet.

4. Bake 10–12 minutes until bottoms are slightly browned. Allow to cool completely on the baking sheet, about 45 minutes.

5. To make Marshmallow: In a small saucepan over medium heat, add sugar and cold water and stir to combine. Bring to a boil, then reduce heat to low and simmer 5 minutes. Remove from heat.

FOR ASSEMBLY

12 tablespoons raspberry jam

2 cups white chocolate chips

1 teaspoon coconut oil

4 drops green gel food coloring

12 teaspoons multicolor ball sprinkles

12 sugar stars

6. Sprinkle gelatin over hot water in a small bowl. Whisk to dissolve gelatin completely. Pour into sugar mixture and stir well. Allow to cool 10 minutes.

7. Pour into bowl of a stand mixer fitted with whisk attachment. Add vanilla and beat on high speed 5–10 minutes until mixture becomes fluffy and has stiff peaks. Scoop Marshmallow into a piping bag fitted with a round tip.

8. To Assemble: Scoop about 1 tablespoon raspberry jam onto center of each cooled Cookie. Pipe Marshmallow in a spiral motion around raspberry jam and continue upward to make a Christmas tree shape. Refrigerate on baking sheet to set, about 30 minutes.

9. Melt white chocolate chips with coconut oil in a small microwave-safe bowl, stirring in 30-second increments until just melted. Add green food coloring and stir to combine. Working quickly, invert each Marshmallow tree on its Cookie base into white chocolate and dip Marshmallow into chocolate. Place back on baking sheet, sprinkle with 1 tablespoon sprinkles, and top with sugar stars. Serve immediately. Leftovers can refrigerated in an airtight container up to 4 days.

S'mores Hot Cocoa

Isle of Java, Disney's Animal Kingdom, Christmas

· · · ✦ · · ·

Isle of Java not only serves yummy coffee drinks all year round; it also has seasonal favorites to check out during certain holidays. And while the temperature doesn't usually get super low in central Florida, it may where you live! A cup of hot cocoa is perfect for a snowy winter day. Just throw a batch together, pop in a movie, grab blankets, and call over some friends!

SERVES 4

3½ cups whole milk

⅓ cup unsweetened cocoa powder

1 cup granulated sugar

⅛ teaspoon salt

⅓ cup water

1 teaspoon vanilla extract

4 ounces toasted marshmallow syrup

½ cup half-and-half

2 cups canned whipped cream

1 graham cracker, finely crushed

1. Combine milk, cocoa powder, sugar, salt, and water in a medium saucepan over medium heat. Stir continuously until well mixed and hot, 3–5 minutes. Remove from heat and stir in vanilla extract and toasted marshmallow syrup.

2. Pour into four mugs. Top each mug with ⅛ cup half-and-half and swirl with whipped cream. Sprinkle on crushed graham cracker and serve immediately.

Disney Parks Tip

Sometimes in the winter, Disney's Animal Kingdom brings out adorable puppets called the "Merry Menagerie" that includes penguins, polar bears, and foxes. Skilled puppeteers let guests interact with the creatures, who really seem like live animals! Catch them on Discovery Island right in front of the Tree of Life.

Holiday Minnie Mouse Bundt Cakes

ABC Commissary, Disney's Hollywood Studios, Christmas

· · · ✳ · · ·

Bundt cakes are so versatile because they have a hole down the middle that you can load up with filling! These bundts are bursting with fun, as they not only have apple pie filling; they are also rolled, drizzled, and topped with festive flavors. If you are enjoying these cakes at ABC Commissary in Disney's Hollywood Studios, be on the lookout for costumes and props from your favorite ABC shows.

MAKES 12 CAKES

FOR SPICED CAKE

1 (13.25-ounce) box spice cake mix

1 cup water

$\frac{1}{3}$ cup vegetable oil

3 large eggs

FOR SPICED MAPLE BUTTERCREAM

$\frac{3}{4}$ cup salted butter, softened

3 cups confectioners' sugar

1 teaspoon vanilla extract

$\frac{1}{8}$ teaspoon maple extract

$\frac{1}{8}$ teaspoon ground cloves

$\frac{1}{8}$ teaspoon ground ginger

$\frac{1}{8}$ teaspoon kosher salt

1 tablespoon heavy whipping cream

1. To make Spiced Cake: Preheat oven to 350°F. Grease a pan with twelve small bundt cake divots with nonstick cooking spray and set aside.

2. In a large bowl, add cake mix, water, vegetable oil, and eggs. Whisk until well combined, about 2 minutes. Pour into bundt cake divots until divots are $\frac{3}{4}$ full. Bake 15–20 minutes until a knife inserted comes out clean. Allow to cool in pan completely, about 45 minutes.

3. To make Spiced Maple Buttercream: Combine all ingredients in bowl of a stand mixer fitted with whisk attachment until creamy and stiff. Scoop into a piping bag fitted with a star attachment and set aside.

FOR ASSEMBLY

- ½ **cup granulated sugar**
- **1 tablespoon ground cinnamon**
- **12 tablespoons apple pie filling**
- **12 tablespoons caramel sauce**
- **1 teaspoon kosher salt**
- **24 (1") milk chocolate disks**
- **12 teaspoons rainbow sprinkles**
- **12 pink candy bows**

4. To Assemble: Stir together sugar and cinnamon in a shallow bowl. Gently roll each Cake in cinnamon sugar and place each on a serving plate.

5. Scoop 1 tablespoon apple pie filling into center hole of each Cake. Drizzle 1 tablespoon caramel sauce on top and sprinkle with kosher salt. Pipe a dollop of Spiced Maple Buttercream over top of hole and place 2 milk chocolate disks on either side of Buttercream to make Mickey ears. Top each Cake with rainbow sprinkles and a candy bow. Serve immediately.

Reindeer Mousse

ABC Commissary, Disney's Hollywood Studios, Christmas

· · · ✦ · · ·

This decadent dessert looks like the most famous reindeer of all: Rudolph! Each November, the ABC Network releases their holiday shows, specials, and movies schedule for December. Almost every day is brimming with delightful favorites, some including *Rudolph the Red-Nosed Reindeer*. When you're tucking into these mousse desserts at home, be sure to queue up this beloved Christmastime classic for the family to watch as you all enjoy every last bite!

SERVES 6

FOR COOKIES

1 cup salted butter, softened

1/2 cup plus 2 tablespoons granulated sugar, divided

1 teaspoon vanilla extract

2 cups all-purpose flour

1 tablespoon gold luster dust

FOR CHOCOLATE MOUSSE

1 1/2 cups heavy whipping cream, divided

1 cup dark chocolate chips

1/2 teaspoon orange extract

1/2 teaspoon cherry extract

1. To make Cookies: Preheat oven to 350°F. Line a half-sized baking sheet with parchment paper and set aside.

2. In bowl of a stand mixer fitted with paddle attachment, cream together butter and 1/2 cup sugar, then add vanilla and flour. Mix until dough is coming together and not crumbly, about 2 minutes.

3. Sprinkle 1 tablespoon sugar across a flat surface and place dough on sugar. Sprinkle top of dough with remaining 1 tablespoon sugar and roll dough out to 1/4" thickness. Use a biscuit cutter or cookie cutter with scalloped edges to cut out 6 (4") circles. Carefully transfer dough circles onto prepared baking sheet. Bake 10–12 minutes until bottoms are slightly browned. Allow to cool completely on baking sheet, about 45 minutes.

4. Once cooled, brush each Cookie with a thin layer of gold luster dust and set aside.

5. To make Chocolate Mousse: Line a jumbo six-divot muffin pan with plastic wrap pushed into each divot. Set aside.

(continued) ▶

FOR DARK CHOCOLATE GLAZE

10 tablespoons salted butter

3/4 cup unsweetened cocoa powder

2 cups confectioners' sugar

2 teaspoons vanilla extract

1/4 cup hot water

FOR CHOCOLATE ANTLERS

1 cup semisweet chocolate chips

1 teaspoon gold luster dust

FOR ASSEMBLY

6 tablespoons canned chocolate buttercream

6 red melting wafers

6. Combine 1/2 cup whipping cream, chocolate chips, and flavored extracts in top of a double boiler. Heat, stirring occasionally, until fully melted (about 5 minutes). Remove from heat and allow to cool, while stirring often, to 85°F (about 10 minutes).

7. In clean bowl of a stand mixer fitted with whisk attachment, beat remaining 1 cup whipping cream until stiff peaks form, about 5 minutes. Fold into cooled chocolate mixture until well combined. Scoop into prepared muffin pan until each divot is full. Refrigerate to set overnight.

8. To make Dark Chocolate Glaze: Melt butter in a small saucepan over medium heat. Add in cocoa powder and stir to combine. Remove from heat. Stir in sugar and vanilla extract. Add in hot water slowly and stir to combine. Remove from heat and allow to cool 15 minutes.

9. To make Chocolate Antlers: Melt semisweet chocolate chips in a small microwave-safe bowl in microwave in 30-second increments until just melted. Quickly scoop into a piping bag with tiny round tip.

10. On a sheet of parchment paper over a half-sized baking sheet, pipe 12 Antler shapes about 2" in height. Refrigerate to set about 30 minutes. Once hard, remove from refrigerator. Brush each with gold luster dust and set aside.

11. To Assemble: Remove Chocolate Mousses from muffin tin and plastic wrap and place on a wire rack. Drizzle Dark Chocolate Glaze over each Chocolate Mousse, making sure top and sides are covered. Refrigerate to set 10 minutes.

12. Carefully scrape glazed Mousses off wire rack and place each onto a gold Cookie. Pipe a dollop of chocolate buttercream on top and place 2 gold Chocolate Antlers on either side of buttercream. Finish with a red melting wafer on front to resemble Rudolph's red nose. Serve immediately or refrigerate in an airtight container up to 3 days.

CHAPTER 7

Disney California Adventure

Disney California Adventure, the epicenter of culinary adventures, takes center stage in this chapter! Much like EPCOT, this Park celebrates a plethora of holidays throughout the year, with a special focus on those closest to the hearts of Californians, whose state is home to a large population of immigrants from Asian and Hispanic countries. The iconic Lunar New Year celebration holds a unique place in this Park, with eye-grabbing red and gold decorations and a cultural extravaganza you won't find at any other Disney Park. Re-create delightful bites like the Mickey Mouse–Shaped Hot Dog Bun, Green Tea Horchata, and Almond Cookie Churros, each bursting with flavor and tradition.

But the party doesn't stop there! This chapter also includes popular treats for Easter, the Fourth of July, Halloween, Christmas, and Hanukkah. Craving a patriotic punch? Don't miss Experiment 0341: Red, White, and Blue Slush from Pym Test Kitchen in Avengers Campus. And if you're brave enough, the spicy Ghost Pepper Potato Bites from Studio Catering Co. served during Oogie Boogie Bash will set your taste buds ablaze. Disney California Adventure knows how to satisfy cravings, and their holiday offerings are no exception.

CARS LAND

PACIFIC WHARF

Flo's V8 Cafe

AVENGER'S CAMPUS

HOLLYWOOD LAND

BUENA VISTA STREET

PIXAR PIER

PARADISE GARDENS
PARK

GRIZZLY PEAK

DISNEY CALIFORNIA ADVENTURE

1. **PORK AND SHRIMP WONTONS WITH A BLACK GARLIC SAUCE** *(Wrapped with Love, Lunar New Year)*

2. **GARLIC NOODLES** *(Longevity Noodle Co., Lunar New Year)*

3. **GREEN TEA HORCHATA** *(Cappuccino Cart, Lunar New Year)*

4. **SESAME SEED DONUTS** *(Lamplight Lounge, Lunar New Year)*

5. **MICKEY MOUSE–SHAPED HOT DOG BUNS** *(Bamboo Blessings, Lunar New Year)*

6. **SURF & TURF FRIED RICE** *(Lamplight Lounge, Lunar New Year)*

7. **ALMOND COOKIE CHURROS** *(Goofy's Churro Cart, Lunar New Year)*

8. **WHITE CHOCOLATE & COCONUT BUNNY RICE CRISPY TREATS** *(Bing Bong's Sweet Stuff, Easter)*

9. **EXPERIMENT 0341: RED, WHITE, AND BLUE SLUSH** *(Pym Test Kitchen, Fourth of July)*

10. **PUMPKIN-SPICED HORCHATA COLD BREW** *(Cappuccino Cart, San Fransokyo Square, Halloween)*

11. **PUMPKIN BUNDT CAKES** *(Cappuccino Cart, San Fransokyo Square, Halloween)*

12. **GHOST PEPPER POTATO BITES** *(Studio Catering Co., Halloween)*

13. **PASTRAMI REUBEN DOG** *(Award Wieners, Hanukkah)*

14. **HOLIDAY MILK MARSHMALLOW WAND** *(Bing Bong's Sweet Stuff, Christmas)*

Pork and Shrimp Wontons with a Black Garlic Sauce

Wrapped with Love, Lunar New Year

· · · ✦ · · ·

Even if you are not normally a seafood person or don't often reach for shrimp, this dish is non-shrimpy-flavored. The shrimp simply adds to the depth of flavor in the wonton filling. Of course, you are always welcome to omit it! After you grab your wontons, head over to San Fransokyo Square and have a meet and greet with Baymax. Just don't try to share a bite of wontons: He doesn't have a mouth!

MAKES ABOUT 40 WONTONS

FOR WONTONS
- ½ **pound ground pork**
- ½ **pound peeled, deveined, and finely chopped raw jumbo shrimp**
- **2 green onions, diced**
- ½ **teaspoon ground black pepper**
- **1 teaspoon salt**
- **2 teaspoons minced garlic**
- **1 teaspoon minced ginger**
- **1 tablespoon sesame oil**
- **1 tablespoon rice vinegar**
- **2 tablespoons soy sauce**
- **1 tablespoon granulated sugar**
- **40 (3") square wonton wrappers**

1. To make Wontons: Set a medium pot of water to boil over medium heat.

2. In a large bowl, combine ground pork, chopped shrimp, green onions, pepper, salt, garlic, ginger, sesame oil, rice vinegar, soy sauce, and sugar.

3. Lay one wonton wrapper in front of you. Scoop 1 teaspoon of filling into center of wrapper. Run a wet finger along entire perimeter of wrapper. Bring opposite sides of wrapper up over filling to meet one another and pinch together. Make sure filling is entirely pinched within the wrapper.

4. Once water is boiling, reduce heat to medium-low to keep water at a low boil. Cook 5–6 Wontons at the same time in boiling water 3–4 minutes until they float to the top. Remove from water with a slotted spoon to a plate and continue wrapping and boiling remaining Wontons.

(continued) ▶

FOR BLACK GARLIC SAUCE

¼ cup soy sauce

2 tablespoons rice vinegar

1 tablespoon sesame oil

2 tablespoons honey

3 cloves black garlic, minced

1 tablespoon diced green onion

5. To make Black Garlic Sauce: Combine all ingredients into a medium bowl. Serve in small bowls alongside Wontons for dipping.

Cooking Hack

If shrimp isn't your thing, replace it with another ½ pound of ground pork. Another ingredient you may choose to sub-out is the black garlic in the dipping sauce. Black garlic can be hard to come by; if you are having trouble finding it, just use regular garlic cloves instead at the same quantity.

Garlic Noodles

Longevity Noodle Co., Lunar New Year

· · · ✦ · · ·

As the name of the restaurant suggests, noodles in Chinese culture are seen as a symbol of longevity. Sometimes on birthdays in China, very long noodles are eaten extra slowly to show how long that person has lived and will live. Instead of your usual noodle dish, try making these Garlic Noodles this week and ponder how long and wonderful your life has been and will be!

SERVES 6

4 tablespoons salted butter

1 teaspoon minced garlic

1 pound spaghetti noodles, cooked al dente

1/2 cup grated Parmesan cheese, divided

1/2 teaspoon ground black pepper

1/2 teaspoon salt

1. In a large saucepan or wok, melt butter and add minced garlic. Cook 2 minutes. Add spaghetti noodles, 1/4 cup Parmesan cheese, pepper, and salt. Stir well to combine.

2. Divide into six serving bowls and top with remaining 1/4 cup Parmesan cheese. Serve immediately.

Disney Parks Tip

Across from Longevity Noodle Co., sometimes you can view World of Color, a nighttime spectacular filled with music, projections, and water effects. It is a very good life indeed, watching World of Color—ONE and slurping Garlic Noodles!

Green Tea Horchata

Cappuccino Cart, Lunar New Year

· · · ✳ · · ·

Just like the blank canvas that is the churro, horchata has been moving up in the ranks as the go-to mix-in for Disneyland seasonal creations. Its neutral flavor profile but distinctive cinnamon pop make it a favorite not only for Latin American communities but also for anyone who loves a refreshing beverage. Green tea brings the East over to the West and is the perfect pairing to celebrate Lunar New Year. Pick this drink up on your way into Pixar Pier or enjoy it at home any time the mood strikes.

SERVES 1

6 ounces prepared horchata

4 ounces prepared chilled green tea

2 cups ice, divided

2 tablespoons white popping boba

Place horchata, green tea, and $\frac{1}{2}$ cup ice into a cocktail shaker and shake until well combined. Strain into an 18-ounce plastic cup and fill with remaining $1\frac{1}{2}$ cups ice until cup is full. Top with boba balls. Add a large-gauge straw and serve immediately.

Cooking Tip

Horchata can typically be found in US grocery stores, either in the chilled juice section or in concentrate form in the international aisle.

Sesame Seed Donuts

Lamplight Lounge, Lunar New Year

· · · ✦ · · ·

Lamplight Lounge is a fan favorite at Disney California Adventure for their yummy eats (including seasonal choices like these donuts) and their Pixar-inspired decor. Concept art and mementos from Pixar movies and shorts adorn the walls. And while they only have these Sesame Seed Donuts during Lunar New Year, don't worry: You can make them any day at home!

MAKES 12 DONUTS

FOR SESAME BRITTLE

2½ tablespoons salted butter
½ cup granulated sugar
⅛ teaspoon salt
½ cup white sesame seeds

FOR KAYA JAM DIPPING SAUCE

½ cup coconut cream
⅓ cup granulated sugar
⅓ cup coconut palm sugar
2 large egg yolks
½ cup heavy whipping cream

FOR ASSEMBLY

12 mini glazed donuts
2 tablespoons maple syrup

1. To make Sesame Brittle: Line a half-sized baking sheet with parchment paper and set aside.

2. In a medium saucepan over medium-high heat, add butter, sugar, and salt. Stir until butter and sugar melt and become liquid. Place a candy thermometer in the mixture and allow to come to 290°F without stirring (7–10 minutes).

3. Remove from heat and stir in sesame seeds, then pour quickly onto prepared baking sheet, smoothing into a uniform ⅛" thickness. Allow to cool completely on the pan, about 1 hour.

4. Break cooled Brittle into chunks and place in a large zip-top bag. Use a rolling pin to smash brittle into a medium-fine dust. Set aside.

5. To make Kaya Jam Dipping Sauce: In a medium saucepan over medium heat, add coconut cream, granulated sugar, and coconut palm sugar. Cook until warmed through, 3–4 minutes.

(continued) ▶

6. Place egg yolks in a medium bowl and scoop about ¼ cup of the sugar mixture slowly into egg yolks while beating continuously. Repeat until all sugar mixture is in egg yolk bowl.

7. Pour back into saucepan, reduce heat to low, and cook 5 minutes to thicken. Add whipping cream and cook 2 minutes more, then remove from heat and pour into small dipping cups.

8. To Assemble: Place donuts in a large bowl and drizzle with maple syrup, tossing to coat. Sprinkle on desired amount of Sesame Brittle dust and toss to coat. Transfer donuts to a serving plate and dip in Kaya Jam Dipping Sauce to enjoy.

Mickey Mouse–Shaped Hot Dog Buns

Bamboo Blessings, Lunar New Year

· · · ✦ · · ·

No, these aren't the hot dog buns that you'd find at a ball game: These are the fluffy, yeasty buns that you'd find in Asian cuisine. Disney chefs took this nod to the Lunar New Year one cute notch up when they shaped the buns like the beloved mouse! Traditional Asian buns may be filled with pork, seafood, or even sweet fillings of red bean or custard. Try filling them with whatever your heart desires.

MAKES 8 BUNS

1 cup bread flour
1 cup all-purpose flour
¼ cup granulated sugar
½ teaspoon salt
1 teaspoon instant yeast
1 tablespoon low-fat milk powder
1 cup plus 1 tablespoon whole milk, divided
⅓ cup heavy whipping cream
1 large egg
8 pork hot dogs
1 large egg yolk
1 tablespoon white sesame seeds
1 tablespoon freeze-dried green onions

1. In bowl of a stand mixer fitted with dough hook attachment, add flours, sugar, salt, yeast, and milk powder. Mix 1 minute. Add in 1 cup whole milk, whipping cream, and egg and knead in mixer 10 minutes or until dough is soft and elastic. Remove from mixer and cover with a clean cloth in a warm place 1–2 hours until dough doubles in size.

2. Preheat oven to 350°F. Line a full-sized baking sheet with parchment paper and set aside.

3. Turn dough out onto a lightly floured surface. Roll out to about ½" thickness. Cut out 8 classic three-circle Mickey head shapes about 5" in diameter. Cut each hot dog into 5 pieces and place hot dog pieces flat side down onto Mickey shapes (1 in each "ear" and 3 in center "face").

4. Mix egg yolk and remaining 1 tablespoon whole milk in a small bowl and brush on buns. Discard extra. Sprinkle buns with sesame seeds and place on baking sheet. Bake 20–25 minutes until buns are golden brown. Remove from oven and sprinkle with green onions. Serve immediately.

Surf & Turf Fried Rice

Lamplight Lounge, Lunar New Year

· · · ✳ · · ·

The age-old question: Seafood or steak? In this dish, you can have both! Flavors of land and sea combine with Asian spices to make a meal sure to satisfy just about everyone. The golden fried rice symbolizes abundance and prosperity for the New Year and is associated with good fortune and wealth. Lunar New Year festivities, spread across Disney California Adventure, are worth seeking out; pair this dish with Sesame Seed Donuts and you're ready to ring in the New Year.

SERVES 1

FOR GINGER PEA PURÉE

- ½ **cup canned sweet peas, drained, liquid reserved**
- ½ **teaspoon minced garlic**
- ¼ **teaspoon minced ginger**
- 1 **tablespoon olive oil**
- 1 **teaspoon lemon juice**
- ½ **teaspoon salt**

FOR SURF & TURF

- 2 **tablespoons salted butter, divided**
- 2 **tablespoons five spice powder, divided**
- 1 **(6-ounce) filet New York strip steak**
- 4 **jumbo shrimp, cleaned with tails on**

1. To make Ginger Pea Purée: Place sweet peas, garlic, ginger, olive oil, lemon juice, and salt in a food processor. Pulse until smooth, adding 1 tablespoon retained pea liquid as needed to thin consistency to a thick sauce. Set aside.

2. To make Surf & Turf: Preheat oven to 500°F.

3. Melt 1 tablespoon butter in a medium oven-proof skillet over high heat on stove. Sprinkle 1 tablespoon five spice powder on all sides of steak and place steak in hot butter. Cook 2 minutes without moving, then flip and cook an additional 2 minutes without moving.

4. Carefully place skillet in oven and cook 4–5 minutes until internal temperature reaches 135°F. Remove from oven and cover skillet loosely with aluminum foil to rest 5 minutes before slicing steak across the grain. Set aside.

FOR FRIED RICE

**1 tablespoon salted
butter**

1 large egg

**1 cup day-old cooked
white rice**

1 tablespoon soy sauce

FOR ASSEMBLY

**1 large carrot, peeled and
spiralized**

2 teaspoons chili oil

5. Toss shrimp in remaining 1 tablespoon five spice powder.
   Melt remaining 1 tablespoon butter in skillet over medium
   heat. Cook shrimp 2–3 minutes per side until shrimp is
   pink and cooked through. Remove to a large plate and
   set aside.

6. To make Fried Rice: In a large skillet or wok, melt butter
   over medium heat. Crack egg into butter and scramble to
   cook. Add in rice and soy sauce, then stir and cook until
   rice is warmed, about 5 minutes. Set aside.

7. To Assemble: Mix together spiralized carrot and chili oil in
   a small bowl and set aside.

8. Spread Ginger Pea Purée in a circle around bottom of
   a serving plate or shallow bowl. Scoop Fried Rice onto
   center of Purée and top with steak strips and shrimp.
   Finish with carrots on top and serve immediately.

Almond Cookie Churros

Goofy's Churro Cart, Lunar New Year

· · · ✦ · · ·

Right between Goofy's Sky School and the Corn Dog Castle, you can find the Goofy Churro Cart, which serves traditional and seasonal churros. During Lunar New Year, you can sometimes find the Almond Cookie Churro that combines the fried goodness of a churro with the baked delight of an almond cookie. Almonds typically blossom during the Lunar New Year, making them a popular ingredient in festive dishes for this holiday. If you can't find almond cookies at your local grocery store, try an Asian market or an online retailer, or substitute another almond-based cookie, like a biscotti.

MAKES 12 CHURROS

- 1 cup room-temperature water
- 3 tablespoons granulated sugar
- $\frac{1}{2}$ teaspoon salt
- 3 tablespoons plus 48 ounces vegetable oil, divided
- 1 cup all-purpose flour
- 10 (1") almond cookies
- $\frac{1}{2}$ cup salted butter, softened
- $\frac{1}{2}$ teaspoon almond extract
- $\frac{1}{2}$ teaspoon vanilla extract
- $2\frac{1}{2}$ cups confectioners' sugar
- 3 tablespoons whole milk
- 6 tablespoons slivered almonds

1. Line a full-sized baking sheet with parchment paper and a large plate with a paper towel and set aside.

2. In a medium saucepan over medium-high heat, add water, sugar, salt, and 3 tablespoons oil. Stir until mixture reaches a boil, about 4 minutes, then remove from heat. Add flour and stir until combined.

3. Scoop dough into a large piping bag fitted with a large star tip or a churro maker fitted with a large star tip. Let dough cool until you are able to hold bag comfortably, about 3 minutes. Pipe dough in twelve (6") lines onto prepared baking sheet. Freeze sheet of churros to set 15 minutes.

4. Place almond cookies in a large zip-top bag and crush with a rolling pin to a fine powder. Place in a shallow dish and set aside.

5. In bowl of a stand mixer fitted with whisk attachment, cream butter 2 minutes until soft and light. Add in almond and vanilla extracts and mix 1 minute more. Gradually add sugar and milk while continuing to mix. Scoop into a piping bag fitted with a small circle tip and set aside.

6. In a large heavy-bottomed pot over medium-high heat, add remaining 48 ounces oil to a depth of at least 3". Heat until oil reaches 375°F.

7. Carefully slide one churro into hot oil. Flip while frying until golden brown, about 2 minutes total. Remove from oil with tongs to paper towel–lined plate and repeat with remaining churros.

8. While churros are still hot, roll in prepared cookie coating until covered and place on a large serving plate. Drizzle with almond-vanilla icing and sprinkle with slivered almonds. Serve immediately.

White Chocolate & Coconut Bunny Rice Crispy Treats

Bing Bong's Sweet Stuff, Easter

. . . ✦ . . .

If you've got Mickey cookie cutters at home and are wondering if you can use them for anything other than Mickey cookies, you're in luck! The innovative minds in the Disney culinary kitchens have taken a Mickey shape, flipped it, and made it into a "bunny butt"! Kids will love to see these at Easter time. Bing Bong's Sweet Stuff, located along Pixar Pier behind the Pixar Pal-A-Round—Swinging Ferris wheel, has these treats and also fun merch to check out!

MAKES 8 TREATS

3 tablespoons salted butter

1 (10-ounce) package mini marshmallows

7 cups crisp rice cereal

4 cups white chocolate chips

2 teaspoons coconut oil

4 large marshmallows

1/2 cup shredded coconut

8 teaspoons white icing

8 teaspoons pink icing

1. In a large microwave-safe bowl, add butter and mini marshmallows and microwave 2 minutes, stir, and microwave 1 minute more or until marshmallows are all melted. Add in rice cereal and stir well to combine.

2. Line a full-sized baking sheet with parchment paper. Grease a large Mickey cookie cutter thoroughly with nonstick cooking spray. Set cutter on prepared baking sheet and scoop rice cereal mixture into cookie cutter until it is all the way full, pressing down to fill completely. Carefully lift cookie cutter upward, leaving Mickey treat behind on tray. Repeat until all rice cereal mixture is used and makes 8 treats, greasing cutter between each use. Refrigerate to set about 30 minutes.

3. Pour white chocolate chips and coconut oil into a medium clean microwave-safe bowl and microwave in 30-second increments, stirring between each, until chips just melt.

(continued) ▶

4. Carefully dunk top half of prepared Mickey treats into white chocolate and place back on prepared baking sheet, chocolate side up. Cut large marshmallows in half and dunk each into remaining white chocolate, and then roll in shredded coconut. Place coconut-covered marshmallows on center of Mickey's "face" and return sheet to refrigerator another 30 minutes for chocolate to set.

5. Remove sheet from refrigerator and finish treats by drawing a circle on each Mickey "ear" in white icing and a tiny paw print in pink icing inside each circle. Serve immediately or refrigerate in an airtight container up to 3 days.

*See Experiment 0341:
Red, White, and Blue Slush recipe on next page* ▶

Experiment 0341:
Red, White, and Blue Slush

Pym Test Kitchen, Fourth of July

· · · ✦ · · ·

Prepare your taste buds for a scientific sensation! Hank Pym himself couldn't have dreamed up a more dazzling (and delicious) experiment than this patriotic powerhouse; it's the perfect way to spark joy and ignite your Fourth of July celebrations. So put on your lab coat (optional, but encouraged!) and embark on a culinary adventure that's sure to be the star of the barbecue.

SERVES 1

FOR BLUE RASPBERRY SYRUP

1 (0.16-ounce) packet Blue Raspberry Kool-Aid

1 cup granulated sugar

1 cup boiling water

FOR SLUSH

3 cups crushed ice, divided

4 ounces Blue Raspberry Syrup

2 ounces lemon syrup

2 ounces lime syrup

1 tablespoon grenadine

2 tablespoons cherry popping boba balls

1. To make Blue Raspberry Syrup: Combine Blue Raspberry Kool-Aid powder, sugar, and boiling water in a small bowl. Once dissolved, refrigerate 1 hour up to overnight.

2. To make Slush: In the pitcher of a blender, add 1½ cups crushed ice and 4 ounces prepared Blue Raspberry Syrup. (Leftover syrup can be refrigerated up to 1 week.) Blend until smooth and pour into a clear 18-ounce plastic cup. Rinse blender pitcher.

3. In clean blender pitcher, add remaining 1½ cups crushed ice, lemon syrup, and lime syrup. Blend until smooth and pour on top of blue Slush in cup. Top with grenadine and popping boba balls and serve with a large-gauge straw.

Serving Tip

If you want to make this for a crowd, just multiply the recipe by the number of guests you have. Keep the flavors separate in chilled pitchers and allow your guests to layer the drink themselves.

Pumpkin-Spiced Horchata Cold Brew

Cappuccino Cart, San Fransokyo Square, Halloween

· · · ✦ · · ·

So many people get excited for PSL (pumpkin spice latte) season to begin in the fall, but this drink takes it to another level with the addition of creamy horchata. Especially attractive for those who are lactose intolerant, horchata is naturally dairy free since it is made from rice milk instead of cow's milk. Notes of cinnamon and nutmeg will dance on your tongue!

SERVES 1

6 ounces prepared horchata

$\frac{1}{8}$ teaspoon pumpkin pie spice

4 ounces prepared cold brew coffee

2 cups ice, divided

Place horchata, pumpkin pie spice, cold brew coffee, and $\frac{1}{2}$ cup ice into a cocktail shaker and shake until well combined. Strain into an 18-ounce plastic cup and fill with remaining $1\frac{1}{2}$ cups ice until cup is full. Serve immediately.

Disney Parks Tip

Check out all the fun Día de los Muertos activities at Disney California Adventure in the Plaza de Familia during the fall months. There are often free crafts for the kids to enjoy as well as special live shows!

Pumpkin Bundt Cakes

Cappuccino Cart, San Fransokyo Square, Halloween

. . . ✳ . . .

The Cappuccino Cart is across the bridge and near the main walkway through the center of Disney California Adventure. Which becomes *very* important to know during Oogie Boogie Bash when you want to get a snack *and* hold your spot for the Frightfully Fun Parade that marches right down that pathway. Here is a hot tip: Grab a spot right near the Cappuccino Cart and you can keep ordering Pumpkin Bundt Cakes and Pumpkin-Spiced Horchata Cold Brews all the way through the parade! It's the perfect setup!

MAKES 18 CAKES

FOR CAKES

- 1 cup salted butter, melted
- 1 (15-ounce) can pumpkin purée
- 3 large eggs
- 2 cups all-purpose flour
- 1½ cups granulated sugar
- 1 teaspoon baking soda
- 2 teaspoons baking powder
- 1 teaspoon ground cinnamon
- 1 teaspoon pumpkin pie spice
- ½ teaspoon salt
- 4 drops orange food coloring

1. To make Cakes: Preheat oven to 350°F. Grease mini bundt pans with nonstick cooking spray and set aside.

2. In bowl of a stand mixer fitted with paddle attachment, add melted butter and pumpkin purée and mix on low 2 minutes to combine. Add in eggs and beat 1 minute more. While continuing to mix on low, add in flour, sugar, baking soda, baking powder, cinnamon, pumpkin pie spice, salt, and food coloring until no dry pockets remain.

3. Scoop batter into a large piping bag with a round tip and pipe into prepared mini bundt pans up to top of each divot. Bake 15–20 minutes until a knife inserted comes out clean. Remove from oven and allow to cool completely in pans, about 1 hour.

8 ounces cream cheese, softened

$\frac{1}{2}$ cup salted butter, softened

1 (13.4-ounce) can dulce de leche

1 teaspoon vanilla extract

7 cups confectioners' sugar

FOR ASSEMBLY

1 cup semisweet chocolate chips

1 cup green frosting

4. To make Dulce de Leche Cream Cheese Frosting: In clean bowl of a stand mixer fitted with whisk attachment, add cream cheese, butter, dulce de leche, and vanilla. Mix on low 2 minutes. While continuing to mix on low, add in sugar 1 cup at a time until incorporated. Scoop into a large piping bag fitted with a star tip.

5. To Assemble: Place chocolate chips in a small microwave-safe bowl and microwave in 30-second increments until just melted. Scoop into a piping bag with a small round tip. Pipe 2" lines onto a sheet of parchment paper and refrigerate to set 30 minutes to make 18 chocolate "stems."

6. Slice Cakes in half horizontally. Pipe a generous swirl of Dulce de Leche Cream Cheese Frosting onto bottom half and sandwich with top half. Pipe green frosting "leaves" on top of each Cake and finish with a chocolate "stem." Serve immediately or cover and refrigerate up to 4 days.

Ghost Pepper Potato Bites

Studio Catering Co., Halloween

. . . ✦ . . .

The ghost pepper has an average rating of about 1 million Scoville Heat Units on the hotness scale, which makes it about 400 times hotter than Tabasco sauce. But this spooky-sounding dish isn't just about heat; it's big on flavor as well. If spice isn't your style, try scaling back on how much ghost pepper hot sauce you include. Even a small amount will pack a big punch! During Oogie Boogie Bash, the area around Studio Catering Co. is transformed into a "treat trail" where you can pick up several pieces of candy and meet a Disney villain!

SERVES 1

FOR GHOST PEPPER CHEESE SAUCE

- 1 teaspoon salted butter
- 1 teaspoon minced garlic
- 1/3 cup heavy whipping cream
- 1 teaspoon cornstarch
- 1 tablespoon cream cheese
- 3/4 cup sharp Cheddar cheese
- 1 tablespoon ghost pepper hot sauce

FOR ASSEMBLY

- 2 cups cooked potato tots
- 1/4 cup bacon bits
- 2 tablespoons pickled jalapeños

1. To make Ghost Pepper Cheese Sauce: In a small pot over medium heat, melt butter. Add garlic and stir until browned, about 3 minutes. Add whipping cream and cornstarch and simmer 2 minutes.

2. Remove from heat and add in cream cheese and Cheddar cheese and stir until melted and creamy. Stir in ghost pepper hot sauce and set aside.

3. To Assemble: Place potato tots in a medium bowl. Drizzle with Ghost Pepper Cheese Sauce, sprinkle with bacon bits, and top with pickled jalapeños. Serve immediately.

Pastrami Reuben Dog

Award Wieners, Hanukkah

· · · ✦ · · ·

As a part of their "Delivering Holiday Cheer" menu, Award Wieners pays tribute to Jewish American communities by piling pastrami high on top of their famous hot dogs. Did you know pastrami can be made with many kinds of different meats, but in the US, pastrami is typically made with beef since that is more readily available than lamb? Whatever kind of pastrami you have will taste incredible on this hot dog. Serve with fries or a mandarin orange to complete the in-Park dish.

SERVES 1

FOR CARAMELIZED ONIONS

1 tablespoon olive oil
1/2 medium yellow onion, peeled, halved, and thinly sliced
1/4 teaspoon kosher salt

FOR ASSEMBLY

1 (5") baguette
1 teaspoon olive oil
2 slices provolone cheese
1 (2-ounce) all-beef hot dog
1 kosher dill pickle spear
1 tablespoon pickled cabbage
1/4 cup thin-sliced pastrami
2 tablespoons spicy mustard
2 tablespoons Thousand Island dressing

1. To make Caramelized Onions: Add oil to a large skillet over medium heat. Add onion and stir 5 minutes. Add salt, reduce heat to low, and allow to cook 60 minutes (stirring frequently) while onion softens and caramelizes. Scoop into a small bowl and set aside.

2. To Assemble: Drizzle baguette with olive oil and toast in toaster oven or broiler 2 minutes. Place slices of provolone on baguette and toast 2 minutes more or until cheese is melted.

3. Place hot dog on top of cheese and lay pickle spear alongside hot dog. Scoop on desired amount of Caramelized Onions. Pile on pickled cabbage and pastrami and drizzle with spicy mustard and Thousand Island dressing. Serve immediately.

Holiday Milk Marshmallow Wand

Bing Bong's Sweet Stuff, Christmas

. . . ✳ . . .

Little seems to delight a child as much as marshmallow dipped in chocolate. And this sweet treat is super easy to make at home! Bing Bong's Sweet Stuff has several confectionary cases filled with seasonal and mainstay treats that are always worth checking out. Bing Bong's has the perfect location, as there are midway games right next door that you can play while munching on your snacks. If you're making this treat at home, try adding holiday sprinkles to the chocolate right after you dip the marshmallows for even more Christmas fun.

SERVES 1

1 cup milk chocolate chips
3 large marshmallows
1 tablespoon green icing
1 tablespoon red icing

1. Place chocolate chips in a small microwave-safe bowl and microwave in 30-second increments until chocolate just melts. Stir and allow chocolate to cool to 85°F.

2. Place marshmallows on a skewer or wooden chopstick. Dip marshmallows in cooled chocolate, spinning to coat. Place on a large plate covered in parchment paper and refrigerate to set 20 minutes.

3. Remove from refrigerator and drizzle with colored icings. Serve.

CHAPTER 8

Disney Springs & Downtown Disney District

Disney Springs at Disney World and the Downtown Disney District in California are culinary playgrounds, where Disney's brightest food minds let their imaginations run wild. With a smorgasbord of eateries in every style, the possibilities are endless! It's no surprise this chapter bursts with treats for some wonderful holidays.

Get ready for a rainbow wave of Pride Month delights with the Celebration Sundae's vibrant hues and the majestic Rainbow Layer Cake. On the romantic side, Valentine's Day brings love-infused treats like Little Love Strawberries and the Love Potion—perfect for a Disney Springs–inspired date night. And May the Fourth be with you at Downtown Disney with both Light and Dark Classic Shakes for your inner Jedi (or Sith!), and Grogu Apples (possibly the cutest treat in the galaxy!). No matter the celebration, Disney Springs and Downtown Disney District always have something special brewing. So grab your appetite and turn the page: Adventure (and deliciousness) awaits!

DISNEY SPRINGS

1 LOVE POTION
(Vivoli il Gelato, Valentine's Day)

2 LITTLE LOVE STRAWBERRIES
(Amorette's Patisserie, Valentine's Day)

3 STRAWBERRY S'MORE
(The Ganachery, Valentine's Day)

4 KING CAKE ICED COFFEE
(Everglazed Donuts & Cold Brew, Mardi Gras)

5 DUBLIN BURGER
(D-Luxe Burger, St. Patrick's Day)

6 POTS OF GOLD & RAINBOWS
(Salt & Straw, St. Patrick's Day)

7 EASTER BASKET NACHOS
(Swirls on the Water, Easter)

8 CELEBRATION SUNDAES
(Ghirardelli Soda Fountain and Chocolate Shop, Pride Month)

9 RAINBOW LAYER CAKE
(Sprinkles, Pride Month)

10 THANKSGIVING LEFTOVER SANDWICH
(Chef Art Smith's Homecomin', Thanksgiving)

DOWNTOWN DISNEY DISTRICT

1. **POTS OF GOLD & RAINBOWS**
   (Salt & Straw, St. Patrick's Day)

2. **LIGHT CLASSIC SHAKE**
   (Black Tap Craft Burgers & Shakes, May the Fourth)

3. **GROGU APPLES**
   (Marceline's Confectionery, May the Fourth)

4 **DARK CLASSIC SHAKE**
(Black Tap Craft Burgers & Shakes, May the Fourth)

5 **FIRECRACKER HOT LINKS**
(Blue Ribbon Corn Dog, Fourth of July)

6 **CANDY CORN CREAM SODA**
(Jazz Kitchen Coastal Grill and Patio, Halloween)

Love Potion

Vivoli il Gelato, Disney Springs, Valentine's Day

· · · ✳ · · ·

One of the best parts of this float served at Disney Springs is the adorable cup it comes in. It is a typical disposable plastic cup, but it has an illustration of a little heart-shaped vial that says "Be Mine." If you want to add this special touch at home, simply use an art vinyl cutter to make a design of your choice. You can also grab any Valentine stickers from the store and add one (or a bunch!) to the outside of the cup to impress your Valentine's date!

SERVES 1

2 cups vanilla gelato

6 ounces Fanta Strawberry

½ cup canned whipped cream

1 teaspoon red sugar sprinkles

In a 16-ounce plastic cup or glass, scoop vanilla gelato. Slowly pour Fanta Strawberry over gelato and top with a swirl of whipped cream and red sprinkles. Serve immediately.

Disney Parks Tip

Vivoli il Gelato is located near the World of Disney store, which has the largest collection of Disney merchandise in the world. What better Valentine's date than getting your sweetheart a Love Potion float and taking them on a shopping spree? Sounds like true love!

Little Love Strawberries

Amorette's Patisserie, Disney Springs, Valentine's Day

· · · ✦ · · ·

Not only is the name of this treat perfectly fitting for Valentine's Day but *Amorette* in French means "Little Love"! So every day is full of love for Amorette's Patisserie. Covered in three different kinds of chocolate, these strawberries will quickly find their way into your lover's heart for Valentine's Day. But don't limit yourself to treating your special someone only on Valentine's Day—you can make these decadent strawberries on any day! Celebrate the "little loves" of your life as often as possible.

MAKES 9 STRAWBERRIES

1 cup white chocolate melting wafers

9 large fresh strawberries, stems on

½ cup ruby chocolate melting wafers

½ cup strawberry chocolate melting wafers

1 tablespoon edible gold flakes

1. Line a half-sized baking sheet with parchment paper and set aside.

2. Place white chocolate melting wafers in a small microwave-safe bowl and microwave 30 seconds on half power. Stir. Repeat cooking and stirring until completely melted.

3. Dip each strawberry completely in white chocolate, leaving stem clean. Place on prepared baking sheet. Refrigerate 30 minutes or until completely hard and no longer wet.

4. Place ruby chocolate melting wafers in a small microwave safe-bowl and microwave 30 seconds on half power. Stir. Repeat cooking and stirring until completely melted.

5. Dip each strawberry in ruby chocolate, only dipping one side of strawberry, at an angle. Place back on prepared baking sheet and refrigerate 30 minutes or until completely hard and no longer wet.

6. Place strawberry chocolate melting wafers in a small microwave-safe bowl and microwave 30 seconds on half power. Stir. Repeat cooking and stirring until completely melted.

7. Dip each strawberry in strawberry chocolate, only dipping opposite side of strawberry, at an angle. Place back on prepared baking sheet and refrigerate 30 minutes or until completely hard and no longer wet.

8. Brush a small amount of water in a line where strawberry and white chocolates meet. Sprinkle water with edible gold flakes. Let dry 10 minutes before serving. Refrigerate leftovers in an airtight container up to 3 days.

Cooking Hack

Ruby chocolate was only introduced in 2017 (as opposed to milk chocolate in 1875), so finding it on shelves at the grocery store might be challenging, though many online retailers now carry it. If you can't find it online, simply use white chocolate dyed with a bit of pink gel food coloring for the same visual effect.

Strawberry S'more

The Ganachery, Disney Springs, Valentine's Day

· · · ✳ · · ·

S'mores are a beloved fireside snack. The Ganachery decided to "elevate" this experience by using chocolate sauce instead of a bar to ensure even chocolaty distribution and a square marshmallow to get gooey goodness all the way to each corner. Lastly, freeze-dried strawberries not only give an adorable look your special someone will enjoy; they also lend a hint of strawberry flavor to each bite. If you don't want to make a heart stencil for this recipe, simply dust the entire top of the s'more with freeze-dried strawberry powder and enjoy.

SERVES 1

¼ cup freeze-dried strawberries

2 graham cracker squares

2 tablespoons chocolate sauce

1 large square marshmallow

1. In bowl of a food processor, pulse freeze-dried strawberries until they are fine dust. Pour into a small bowl and set aside.

2. Place graham crackers on a small plate and drizzle each on one side with chocolate sauce.

3. Place marshmallow square on a skewer and use a gas-fire kitchen stove or kitchen torch to toast all sides of marshmallow until golden brown and fluffy. Place marshmallow on top of one chocolate-covered graham cracker. Flip over second graham cracker so chocolate is facing marshmallow and place on top.

4. Take a piece of cardstock paper the size of a graham cracker square and cut out several small hearts. Place paper on top of graham cracker and dust freeze-dried strawberry powder over paper. Lift paper to reveal heart shapes on cracker. Enjoy immediately.

King Cake Iced Coffee

Everglazed Donuts & Cold Brew, Disney Springs, Mardi Gras

· · · ✦ · · ·

Everglazed Donuts & Cold Brew, an amazing donut and coffee shop tucked next to the AMC Theater at Disney Springs, has only been open since 2021. It specializes in over-the-top beverages. This festive drink features the fun colors and flavors of Mardi Gras, and you can feel free to adjust the sweetness level to your liking by adding more or less sweetened condensed milk.

SERVES 1

- **8 ounces prepared dark roast coffee**
- **1 tablespoon sweetened condensed milk**
- **1 tablespoon caramel syrup**
- **1/8 teaspoon ground cinnamon**
- **1/4 cup canned whipped cream**
- **1/4 teaspoon purple sugar sprinkles**
- **1/4 teaspoon green sugar sprinkles**
- **1/4 teaspoon yellow sugar sprinkles**

In an 18-ounce plastic cup or glass, add ice to fill, then pour coffee over ice. Add sweetened condensed milk, caramel syrup, and cinnamon and stir well to combine. Top with a swirl of whipped cream and finish with colored sprinkles. Serve immediately.

Dublin Burger

D-Luxe Burger, Disney Springs, St. Patrick's Day

. . . ✦ . . .

Ireland is known for its dairy products (like the Irish cheese in this recipe) due to its lush grass for grazing, so sheep and cows produce delicious milk. And Guinness is an easily accessible Irish stout in the United States, but feel free to use any dark beer you prefer to make the barbecue sauce.

SERVES 1

FOR IRISH STOUT BARBECUE SAUCE

- 11.2 ounces Irish stout beer
- ½ cup light brown sugar
- ¾ cup ketchup
- 1 tablespoon apple cider vinegar
- 4 tablespoons honey
- 1 teaspoon garlic powder
- 1 teaspoon ground black pepper

FOR ASSEMBLY

- 2 (¼-pound) ground beef patties
- 2 slices Irish Cheddar cheese
- 1 tablespoon salted butter, softened
- 1 brioche hamburger bun
- 2 leaves butter lettuce
- 2 thin slices corned beef
- 2 tablespoons crispy fried onions

1. To make Irish Stout Barbecue Sauce: In a large saucepan over medium-high heat, add Irish stout beer. Bring to a boil, then lower heat to medium and allow beer to simmer until reduced by half, about 15 minutes.

2. Add brown sugar, ketchup, apple cider vinegar, honey, garlic powder, and pepper and stir to combine. Reduce heat to low and simmer until thickened, about 5 minutes. Remove from heat and refrigerate 1 hour, up to 2 weeks.

3. To Assemble: Spray a grill pan with nonstick cooking spray and place beef patties on pan. Allow to cook 5 minutes, then flip and use spatula to press burgers to a ½" thickness. Allow to cook 3–5 minutes more until meat reaches an internal temperature of 160°F. Place Cheddar cheese slices on each patty and let melt, 1–2 minutes. Remove from pan to a plate.

4. Spread butter on inside surfaces of brioche bun and place on grill pan to brown, 2–3 minutes. Remove from pan and place on serving plate.

5. Start with bottom of brioche bun, then add lettuce leaves, both burger patties (with cheese on them), corned beef slices, and crispy fried onions. Drizzle with Irish Stout Barbecue Sauce. Serve immediately.

Pots of Gold & Rainbows

Salt & Straw, Disney Springs and Downtown Disney District, St. Patrick's Day

. . . ✳ . . .

Salt & Straw is originally a Portland, Oregon, institution but has now opened locations across the country, including Disney Springs in Florida and Downtown Disney in California. Salt & Straw serves this ice cream exclusively during the St. Patrick's Day season, but you can make it any day of the year with this easy recipe. Lucky Charms is a popular cereal all year round in American households, but its mascot, a jovial leprechaun, makes the cereal an excellent St. Patrick's Day treat!

SERVES 4

1½ cups whole milk

1 cup heavy whipping cream

1 cup Lucky Charms cereal

1 tablespoon cream cheese

⅓ cup granulated sugar

1 teaspoon vanilla extract

½ cup Lucky Charms marshmallows

4 waffle cones

1. In a large measuring cup, add milk and whipping cream. Pour in Lucky Charms cereal and stir to wet. Refrigerate 4 hours up to overnight.

2. In a large microwave-safe bowl, add cream cheese and microwave 30 seconds. Add sugar and vanilla extract and stir until a frosting-like consistency forms.

3. Pour cereal, milk, and whipping cream mixture through a strainer to collect 1¾ cups cereal milk. Discard excess. Add cereal milk to sugar–cream cheese mixture and whisk well to combine.

4. Pour into an ice cream machine and run according to manufacturer's instructions, 15–20 minutes until creamy. Scoop into a freezer container and fold in Lucky Charms marshmallows. Allow to set in freezer an additional 1–4 hours until mixture reaches desired consistency. Scoop into waffle cones and serve.

Light Classic Shake

Black Tap Craft Burgers & Shakes, Downtown Disney District, May the Fourth

· · · ✦ · · ·

Black Tap Craft Burgers & Shakes is a New York City–based restaurant chain known for its over-the-top milkshakes. Their shakes are made with high-quality ingredients and topped with all sorts of delicious treats. The "light side" of the Force in the Star Wars universe is characterized by compassion, peace, and justice. Jedi Knights who follow the light side of the Force often wield blue lightsabers. The Light Classic Shake is a yummy way to celebrate the light side of the Force.

SERVES 1

3 cups vanilla ice cream
½ cup whole milk
2 drops blue liquid food coloring
2 tablespoons chocolate syrup, divided
½ cup canned whipped cream
1 tablespoon blue and silver sprinkles

1. In the pitcher of a blender, add vanilla ice cream, milk, and blue food coloring. Blend until well combined.

2. Prepare a milkshake glass by drizzling 1 tablespoon chocolate syrup around inside of glass. Pour milkshake into glass. Top with whipped cream and drizzle with remaining 1 tablespoon chocolate syrup. Top with sprinkles. Serve immediately.

Grogu Apples

Marceline's Confectionery, Downtown Disney District, May the Fourth

. . . ✦ . . .

Baby Yoda mania has taken over the world—and also Disney Parks! These candy apples are fun to buy at Marceline's Confectionery, where you can watch them being made in the front window. However, they can also be found in candy displays across the Disneyland Resort, as well as across the country at the Walt Disney World Resort! Make them as detailed or simple as you please; as long as you can tell they resemble everyone's favorite space baby, it's up to you!

MAKES 4 APPLES

4 extra-large Granny Smith apples

1 (11-ounce) bag caramel bits

2 tablespoons water

30 ounces vanilla-flavored melting wafers, divided

2 drops green gel food coloring

4 large marshmallows

2 drops brown gel food coloring

4 teaspoons white icing, divided

4 tablespoons brown sanding sugar

4 teaspoons black piping icing

1. Line a full-sized baking sheet with parchment paper sprayed with cooking oil. Set aside.

2. Drive a dowel or Popsicle stick into top of each apple. Place caramel bits and water in a medium microwave-safe bowl and microwave 2 minutes and stir. If not melted entirely, microwave an additional 30 seconds and stir. Dip each apple in melted caramel, tipping apple and bowl to allow caramel to cover entire apple. Allow excess caramel to drip off, then scrape excess off bottom. Place apples on prepared baking sheet and refrigerate 1 hour.

3. Place 20 ounces vanilla-flavored melting wafers into a small microwave-safe bowl and microwave on 50% power 1 minute, then stir. Continue cooking and stirring until wafers are completely melted. Add green food coloring and stir to combine.

4. Use kitchen shears to cut large marshmallows diagonally. Take flat side of one marshmallow half (not cut edge) and dip into melted wafers. Firmly stick to one side of one apple. Repeat dipping with other marshmallow half and stick to other side of same apple. Repeat with remaining marshmallows and apples to give each apple Grogu "ears."

5. Carefully dip each apple into melted wafers, tipping apple and bowl to allow wafers to cover entire apple, including ears. Scrape excess off bottom back into bowl and return apples to prepared baking sheet. Refrigerate 30 minutes.

6. Place remaining 10 ounces melting wafers in a clean microwave-safe bowl and microwave on 50% power 1 minute, then stir. Continue until wafers are completely melted. Add brown food coloring and stir to combine. Dip bottom half of each apple into brown melted wafers, return to baking pan and refrigerator another 30 minutes.

7. Use tube of white icing to trace a line between green and brown sections of apple and sprinkle with brown sanding sugar. Finish by drawing, then filling in circles for eyes with black icing and use remaining white icing to dot each eye, fill in ears, and make a nose. Refrigerate to set 30 minutes, then serve.

Dark Classic Shake

Black Tap Craft Burgers & Shakes, Downtown Disney District, May the Fourth

· · · ✳ · · ·

In literal contrast to the Light Classic Shake, the Dark Classic Shake is for all the fans of the "dark," or Sith, side of the Force. This shake is eye grabbing with red and black hues and recalls characters who display these colors, like Darth Maul and Darth Vader. Don't worry, no one will think you're flipping to the dark side if you make this at home—they will just assume that you love the incredible combination of cherry and chocolate!

SERVES 1

3 cups vanilla ice cream

½ cup whole milk

5 tablespoons maraschino cherry juice

1 drop red liquid food coloring

2 tablespoons chocolate syrup, divided

½ cup canned whipped cream

1 tablespoon red and black sprinkles

1 maraschino cherry, stem on

1. In the pitcher of a blender, add vanilla ice cream, milk, cherry juice, and red food coloring. Blend until well combined.

2. Prepare a milkshake glass by drizzling 1 tablespoon chocolate syrup around inside of glass. Pour milkshake into glass. Top with whipped cream and drizzle with remaining 1 tablespoon chocolate syrup. Top with sprinkles and cherry. Serve immediately.

Easter Basket Nachos

Swirls on the Water, Disney Springs, Easter

· · · ✦ · · ·

Swirls on the Water always has the best and latest Dole Whip flavors in such fun configurations! And these Easter Basket Nachos are truly one of the best creations that they serve. Grab the large pieces of waffle cone and dunk them in the soft-serve and sorbet like chips in nachos. The playful pink and blue colors, along with the pop of fun and flavor from the jelly beans, make this recipe a hopping good time.

SERVES 1

FOR COTTON CANDY SOFT-SERVE

1 tablespoon cream cheese

1/3 cup blue raspberry cotton candy sugar

1 tablespoon cotton candy syrup

3/4 cup heavy whipping cream

1 cup whole milk

FOR RASPBERRY SORBET

4 1/2 cups fresh raspberries

1/4 cup granulated sugar

1. To make Cotton Candy Soft-Serve: In a large microwave-safe bowl, add cream cheese and microwave 30 seconds. Add cotton candy sugar and cotton candy syrup and stir until a frosting-like consistency forms. Pour in whipping cream and milk and stir to combine. Pour into an ice cream machine and run according to manufacturer's instructions, 15–20 minutes until creamy. Scoop into a freezer container and set aside in freezer.

2. To make Raspberry Sorbet: Add raspberries and sugar to a blender or food processor and blend until smooth. Add 1 tablespoon water at a time if mixture is too thick to blend. Pour through a medium-mesh sieve to remove seeds, then pour into an ice cream machine and run according to manufacturer's instructions, 15–20 minutes until creamy.

(continued) ▶

2 waffle cones, broken into pieces

¼ cup canned whipped cream

2 tablespoons assorted jelly beans

1 tablespoon raspberry sauce

3. To Assemble: Place waffle cone pieces into bottom of a serving bowl. Squirt canned whipped cream onto cone pieces. Scoop Cotton Candy Soft-Serve and Raspberry Sorbet onto whipped cream (leftover Soft-Serve and Sorbet can be frozen in airtight containers up to 2 weeks). Sprinkle with jelly beans and drizzle with raspberry sauce. Serve immediately.

Serving Tip

At Swirls on the Water, both flavors of frozen dessert are swirled together right out of the soft-serve machine! And while scooping them separately at home is perfectly acceptable, if you want to achieve the same look, simply scoop both flavors side by side into a large piping bag fitted with a star tip and squeeze out quickly onto the whipped cream.

Celebration Sundaes

Ghirardelli Soda Fountain and Chocolate Shop, Disney Springs, Pride Month

· · · ✦ · · ·

Even though this colorful sundae was crafted for Pride Month at Disney, you can enjoy it any day, anywhere! In fact, if you aren't in the mood to mix up six different colors for your waffle bowl, feel free to use as many or as few as you like. Pride Month occurs every year in June, and Disney marks the occasion with colorful treats and sweets, as well as photo stops and exclusive merchandise.

SERVES 4

1 large egg white

2 tablespoons heavy cream

¼ cup granulated sugar

⅛ teaspoon salt

½ teaspoon vanilla extract

½ teaspoon almond extract

⅓ cup all-purpose flour

3 tablespoons salted butter, melted

2 drops each red, orange, yellow, green, blue, and purple gel food coloring

1. Preheat waffle cone maker to medium heat.

2. In bowl of a stand mixer fitted with whisk attachment, add egg white and beat 2 minutes on high until foamy. Add in heavy cream, sugar, salt, and vanilla and almond extracts. Whip 2 more minutes. Add flour and whisk 1 additional minute. Slowly add melted butter while whisking and whip 1 more minute or until all is combined. Divide batter equally into six bowls and dye each bowl's batter with a different gel food coloring.

3. Scoop 1 tablespoon of each color of prepared batter onto preheated waffle cone maker in pie-slice shapes. Close and cook 1 minute or until golden brown. Remove and immediately press into a 1-cup heat-resistant bowl and allow to set 5 minutes or until hard. Remove from bowl and set aside. Repeat with remaining batter to make 3 more waffle "bowls."

1 cup hot fudge

6 cups vanilla ice cream

4 cups canned whipped cream

4 teaspoons rainbow sprinkles

4 maraschino cherries, stem on

4. When ready to serve, spoon hot fudge into bottom of waffle bowls and scoop in vanilla ice cream. Top with whipped cream, sprinkle with rainbow sprinkles, and finish each sundae with a maraschino cherry.

Rainbow Layer Cake

Sprinkles, Disney Springs, Pride Month

· · · · ✦ · · ·

This cake is super loud and super proud! Six layers of fluffy colorful cake are topped with silky frosting and covered in bright rainbow sprinkles. Everyone at your party will be excited to have a slice—just don't be surprised if they lick their plates clean!

SERVES 8

FOR CAKE

- 2 cups salted butter, softened
- 3½ cups granulated sugar
- 12 large egg whites, room temperature
- 3½ cups all-purpose flour
- 2 tablespoons baking powder
- 2 teaspoons almond extract
- 2 teaspoons vanilla extract
- 2½ cups whole milk
- 4 drops each gel food coloring in red, orange, yellow, green, blue, and purple

1. To make Cake: Preheat oven to 340°F. Prepare six 9" round cake pans with a round piece of parchment paper on the bottom of each pan and grease with nonstick cooking spray around pan's inside edge. Set aside.

2. In bowl of a stand mixer fitted with paddle attachment, cream butter and sugar together on medium speed 3 minutes or until light and fluffy. Add in egg whites slowly and mix 2 minutes on low or until incorporated. Add in flour, baking powder, almond extract, vanilla extract, and milk while mixer is still running. Mix on low 2 minutes more or until a uniform batter forms.

3. Scoop 2 cups each of batter into six separate bowls. Color each bowl of batter with a different gel food coloring color. Each color should be vivid. Scoop colored batters into prepared pans, smoothing each surface. Bake 25–35 minutes until knife inserted in center comes out clean. Remove from oven and allow to cool at room temperature 1 hour.

(continued) ▶

FOR FROSTING

2 cups salted butter, softened

2 pounds confectioners' sugar

1 teaspoon vanilla extract

$\frac{1}{2}$ cup whipping cream

$1\frac{1}{4}$ cups rainbow sprinkles, divided

4. To make Frosting: In a clean stand mixer fitted with whisk attachment, cream butter 3 minutes on medium speed until light and fluffy. Gradually add in confectioners' sugar while mixer is running until all is incorporated, about 2 minutes. Add in vanilla extract and whipping cream and mix 2 minutes more. Pour in 1 cup rainbow sprinkles and mix 1 minute or until just combined.

5. Place purple Cake round on a large plate. Remove parchment paper from Cake back. Spread with a thin layer of Frosting. Repeat with remaining Cakes in reverse color order: purple, blue, green, yellow, orange, then red. Keep sides and edges of Cakes free of frosting. Once all Cakes have been stacked, frost top of cake over red layer. Sprinkle with remaining $\frac{1}{4}$ cup rainbow sprinkles.

6. Slice into 8 slices and serve immediately. Leftover cake can be refrigerated in an airtight container up to 4 days.

See Firecracker Hot Links recipe on next page ▶

Firecracker Hot Links

Blue Ribbon Corn Dog, Downtown Disney District, Fourth of July

· · · · ✦ · · ·

Can you take the heat? This snack stacks spicy on spicy on spicy, from the juicy hot link inside to the sriracha mayo on top and the finishing touch of Flamin' Hot Cheetos. And while Blue Ribbon Corn Dog can't accommodate all requests for customization, at home you can make your Firecracker Hot Link as spicy or mild as you desire. Try swapping out the hot link for a beef frank, or using ketchup mayo instead of sriracha mayo, or regular Cheetos rather than Flamin' Hot.

SERVES 6

48 ounces vegetable oil, for frying

1¼ cups all-purpose flour

2 tablespoons granulated sugar

½ teaspoon salt

2 teaspoons baking powder

½ cup whole milk

1 large egg

1 cup panko bread crumbs

6 hot links

6 tablespoons sriracha mayo

1 (3.25-ounce) bag Flamin' Hot Cheetos, crushed into crumbs

1. Pour oil into a large pot over medium heat and bring to 350°F. Line a large plate with paper towels and set aside.

2. Combine flour, sugar, salt, baking powder, milk, and egg in a medium bowl. Pour batter into a tall drinking glass ¾ full (if it doesn't all fit, refill glass as necessary). Pour panko into a shallow dish.

3. Skewer hot links with wooden chopsticks or Popsicle sticks. Dry each hot link with a paper towel. Dunk skewered hot links, one at a time, in glass of batter, then roll in panko.

4. Carefully lower battered hot links into hot oil (only fry 1 or 2 at a time to avoid dropping oil temperature) and fry 2–3 minutes until golden brown. Repeat for all hot links.

5. Remove hot links from oil onto a paper towel–lined plate. Remove paper towels and squirt sriracha mayo in a zigzag down each hot link and sprinkle with Flamin' Hot Cheetos crumbs. Serve immediately.

Candy Corn Cream Soda

Jazz Kitchen Coastal Grill and Patio, Downtown Disney District, Halloween

. . . ✦ . . .

When Candy Corn Cream Soda was first served at this restaurant, the restaurant was called "Ralph Brennan's Jazz Kitchen," but the name has since changed to "Jazz Kitchen Coastal Grill and Patio." However, it still has the same heart and soul as before—and it updated its popular beignet to-go express window to an adjacent Beignet Expressed venue! Now you can bring the Jazz Kitchen to your own home whenever the craving strikes.

SERVES 1

- **2 ounces Monin Candy Corn Syrup**
- **1 ounce half-and-half**
- **8 ounces club soda**
- **¼ cup canned whipped cream**
- **1 tablespoon candy corn**

In a 16-ounce plastic or glass cup, add syrup and half-and-half and stir well to combine. Slowly add club soda and stir gently to combine. Fill cup with ice cubes, and then top with whipped cream. Sprinkle with candy corn. Serve immediately.

Thanksgiving Leftover Sandwich

Chef Art Smith's Homecomin', Disney Springs, Thanksgiving

. . . ✳ . . .

Of course Chef Art isn't scrounging up Thanksgiving leftovers to make this sandwich, but you can make this at home with food you have on hand. Whatever kind of stuffing you made for Thanksgiving dinner, use that! Did you bake your turkey instead of smoking it? Use that! Whip up a fresh batch of this Cranberry Aïoli to tie it all together.

SERVES 1

FOR CORNBREAD STUFFING

1^1/$_2$ cups water

2 tablespoons butter

1 (6-ounce) box cornbread stuffing mix

FOR CRANBERRY AÏOLI

2 tablespoons cranberry sauce

2 tablespoons mayonnaise

^{1}/$_4$ teaspoon honey Dijon mustard

^{1}/$_8$ teaspoon garlic powder

FOR ASSEMBLY

2 slices thick artisan bread

2 tablespoons salted butter

2 ounces smoked turkey

^{1}/$_2$ teaspoon chopped fresh parsley

1 cup barbecue chips

1. To make Cornbread Stuffing: Bring water and butter to a boil in a medium saucepan over medium heat. Stir in cornbread stuffing mix and cover 5 minutes. Remove lid and fluff with a fork. Set aside.

2. To make Cranberry Aïoli: Whisk together all ingredients in a small bowl. Set aside.

3. To Assemble: Toast slices of bread in a toaster until golden brown, allow to cool 1 minute in toaster, and spread one side of each piece with butter. Lay bread slices with buttered side facing up on a serving plate. Spread a thick layer of Cornbread Stuffing on one slice of bread, stack with smoked turkey, and drizzle with Cranberry Aïoli. Top with second slice of bread, buttered side down. Slice in half and sprinkle tops with chopped fresh parsley. Serve alongside barbecue chips.

CHAPTER 9

Disney Resort Hotels

In this final chapter, get ready to embark on a culinary odyssey across the sprawling magic of *all* the Disney Resort Hotels! These aren't your average bed and breakfasts: With hundreds, even *thousands*, of rooms to fill, they're culinary meccas bursting with diverse dining options. A wide array of holidays are meticulously catered to by the Resort Hotels of Disneyland and Walt Disney World.

Raise a toast to New Year's Eve with the bubbly Champagne Beignets and the shimmering New Year's Float, sure to ignite festive cheer. And brace yourself for a Thanksgiving feast with recipes like the Pumpkin Pie Shake and Butternut Squash Bisque, or the Easter treats of Thumper Carrot Cakes and Peanut Butter Eggs; there's nothing quite like indulging in those holiday delights within the cozy embrace of your own home. So jump aboard the Monorail, swing into a Skyliner gondola, or grab a magical bus—it's time to "Resort hop," savoring every delicious stop along the way!

Berry Beignets

Scat Cat's Club—Lounge, Disney's Port Orleans Resort—French Quarter, Black History Month/Celebrate Soulfully

. . . . ✦ . . .

The whiskey used in this recipe is no ordinary whiskey. It is named for Nathan "Nearest" Green, a former enslaved person who taught Jack Daniel (yes, that Jack Daniel) how to make whiskey. Each batch is aged for a minimum of four years and promises a smooth and complex flavor profile filled with notes of vanilla, caramel, oak, and spice. And while of course you can use any whiskey for this recipe, using Uncle Nearest helps honor the people who endured so much. Serve each irresistible Berry Beignet alongside a scoop of ice cream topped with mint.

SERVES 10

FOR UNCLE NEAREST 1884 SMALL BATCH WHISKEY CARAMEL SAUCE

- 1½ cups granulated sugar
- ¼ cup water
- ½ cup heavy whipping cream
- 4 tablespoons salted butter
- 2½ tablespoons Uncle Nearest 1884 Small Batch Whiskey
- ½ teaspoon vanilla extract

FOR BEIGNETS

- 1½ cups warm water (110°F)
- ½ cup granulated sugar

1. To make Uncle Nearest 1884 Small Batch Whiskey Caramel Sauce: In a large saucepan over medium-high heat, add sugar and water and whisk to combine. Allow to come to a boil, 3–5 minutes. Reduce heat to low and simmer 12–15 minutes until mixture is a dark amber color.

2. Remove from heat and whisk in whipping cream, butter, whiskey, and vanilla extract. Let cool to room temperature, about 1 hour, and pour into a squeeze-tip bottle. Set aside.

3. To make Beignets: In a small bowl, stir water together with sugar and yeast. Let sit 10 minutes. In bowl of a stand mixer fitted with whisk attachment, add eggs and whip 1 minute. Add salt and evaporated milk and whisk 1 minute more. Slowly pour in yeast mixture and stir 1 minute more to combine.

(continued) ▶

1 (¼-ounce) packet
   active dry yeast
2 large eggs
1¼ teaspoons salt
1 cup evaporated milk
7 cups bread flour,
   divided
¼ cup shortening
4 cups vegetable oil for
   frying

FOR BERRY COMPOTE

2 cups fresh
   strawberries, hulled
   and diced
2 cups fresh blueberries
2 tablespoons honey
4 large fresh mint leaves,
   thinly sliced

FOR ASSEMBLY

3 cups confectioners'
   sugar

4. Add 3 cups flour while continuing to mix. Add shortening and remaining 4 cups flour, switching to a dough hook when dough gets too sticky for the whisk. Knead with dough hook 5 minutes or until dough comes together and is elastic.

5. Grease a large bowl and transfer dough to greased bowl. Cover with greased plastic wrap and place in a warm area to rise 3 hours or until dough doubles in size.

6. In a large heavy-bottomed pot over medium-high heat, add vegetable oil. Heat until oil reaches 350°F.

7. Line a half-sized baking sheet with paper towels and set aside.

8. Flour a flat, clean surface and roll dough out to ¼" thickness. Cut into Mickey shapes. Carefully slide 2 or 3 dough Mickeys into the hot oil and fry about 1 minute on each side until golden brown. Transfer to lined baking sheet. Repeat with remaining Mickeys and set aside.

9. To make Berry Compote: In a medium bowl, mix diced strawberries, blueberries, and honey together. Fold in mint leaf slices. Refrigerate 1 hour.

10. To Assemble: Place a scoop of Berry Compote on each serving plate, place one Mickey Beignet on top of berries, sift sugar over Beignets, and drizzle with Uncle Nearest 1884 Small Batch Whiskey Caramel Sauce. Serve immediately. Leftover Caramel Sauce can be refrigerated in an airtight container up to 1 week.

Baked Andouille Mac & Cheese

Hearthstone Lounge, Disney's Grand Californian Hotel & Spa,
Black History Month/Celebrate Soulfully

· · · ✦ · · ·

While Andouille sausage has roots in the French regions of Brittany and Normandy, the French-American settlers and enslaved African Americans of the Louisiana region blended cultures to give Andouille a new spin, stuffing the sausages with delicious chunky fillings of pork, garlic, peppers, onions, and seasonings. Tucked into mac and cheese, the spicy and creamy flavors are a party in your mouth!

SERVES 8

½ cup plus 3 tablespoons salted butter, divided

2 tablespoons all-purpose flour

1 teaspoon garlic powder

½ teaspoon ground white pepper

½ teaspoon salt

½ teaspoon onion powder

2 cups heavy whipping cream

1 (8-ounce) block white Cheddar cheese, shredded

1 pound elbow macaroni, cooked and drained

2 teaspoons dried oregano

2 teaspoons dried parsley

2 Andouille sausage links, sliced

1 cup plain bread crumbs

¼ cup fresh parsley leaves

1. Preheat oven to 350°F. Grease a 9" × 13" baking pan with nonstick cooking spray and set aside.

2. In a medium saucepan, melt ½ cup butter over medium heat. Add flour, garlic powder, white pepper, salt, and onion powder. Stir to combine and cook until golden brown, about 3 minutes. Add heavy cream and whisk until smooth. Stir in shredded cheese and cooked macaroni and stir well.

3. Scoop into prepared pan. Sprinkle with oregano and parsley and tuck Andouille sausage slices into macaroni evenly across pan.

4. In a small microwave-safe bowl, add remaining 3 table-spoons butter and microwave 1 minute to melt. Stir in bread crumbs, then spread across macaroni and bake 15–20 minutes until crumbs are golden and macaroni is bubbly. Scoop into bowls and top with fresh parsley leaves. Serve immediately or refrigerate in an airtight container up to 3 days.

Mickey Shamrock Milk Shake

Beaches & Cream Soda Shop, Disney's Beach Club Resort, St. Patrick's Day

· · · ✳ · · ·

You must be having a lucky day indeed if you're drinking (and eating!) one of these decadent shakes. Beaches & Cream Soda Shop is known for their over-the-top milkshakes served in reusable plastic jars, so next time you dine there, order one and take the jar home with you. Then you can make this Mickey Shamrock Milk Shake right in the original jar.

SERVES 1

FOR MILK SHAKE

- 1 tablespoon chocolate syrup
- 1 tablespoon white frosting
- 1 tablespoon shamrock sprinkles
- 3 cups mint chocolate chip ice cream
- 1/4 cup whole milk
- 1 white cupcake, unwrapped

FOR CHOCOLATE BUCKLE

- 1/4 cup semisweet chocolate chips
- 1 teaspoon gold luster dust

1. To make Milk Shake: Prepare a 16-ounce canning jar by drizzling chocolate syrup around inside of jar. Smear white frosting around outer rim of jar and press shamrock sprinkles into rim. Set aside.

2. In the pitcher of a blender, add mint ice cream and milk and blend until smooth, about 1 minute. Pour into prepared jar until mixture reaches just below jar rim. Place white cupcake on top of Milk Shake.

3. To make Chocolate Buckle: Place chocolate chips in a microwave-safe bowl and microwave in 30-second increments until just melted. Scoop into a piping bag with small round tip. Pipe a 1" buckle shape onto a sheet of parchment paper and place in refrigerator to set 30 minutes. Once set, brush with luster dust.

(continued) ▶

2 tablespoons black frosting

1 tablespoon green frosting

2 chocolate candy melt rounds

1 teaspoon white stick sprinkles

4. To Assemble: Scoop frostings into piping bags fitted with a star tip (additional frosting may be needed in the bag to push frosting out). Swirl a layer of black frosting onto the cupcake, followed by a smaller swirl of green frosting on top of black. Place 2 candy melt rounds on top to resemble mouse ears, place Chocolate Buckle onto front of frosting, and finish with white sprinkles. Serve immediately.

Cooking Hack

One way to make this shake extra fast is to grab premade pouches of frosting at the grocery store that already have star tips attached. You can just pipe on the amount you need for your shake, cap the pouches, and use them the next time you're craving a Mickey Shamrock Milk Shake!

Peanut Butter Eggs

Contempo Café, Disney's Contemporary Resort, Easter

· · · ✦ · · ·

Many people know and love the classic peanut butter eggs sold at the grocery store during Easter season, but have you ever made them at home? They are surprisingly easy! Just a few simple ingredients that you may already have on hand, and you've got yourself a delicious treat. Contempo Café is a pretty small and unassuming hotel café but is viewed by about fifteen million people per year because it can be seen from the Magic Kingdom Monorail.

MAKES 18 "EGGS"

6 tablespoons salted butter, softened

1 cup crunchy peanut butter

2½ cups confectioners' sugar

½ teaspoon vanilla extract

⅛ teaspoon salt

1 (12-ounce) bag semisweet chocolate chips

1 teaspoon coconut oil

½ cup white icing

2 tablespoons rainbow sprinkles

1. Line a half-sized baking sheet with parchment paper and set aside.

2. In bowl of a stand mixer fitted with paddle attachment, add in butter and peanut butter and mix on low until combined, about 2 minutes. Add in sugar, vanilla, and salt. Mix on low 2 minutes more or until well mixed.

3. Using a 1–2 tablespoon cookie scoop, scoop a ball of peanut butter mixture into your hand. Use your hands to mold ball into a flat egg shape, and then place on prepared baking sheet. Repeat with remaining peanut butter mixture to make about 18 "eggs." Refrigerate to set 2 hours.

4. In a medium, microwave-safe bowl, add chocolate chips and coconut oil. Microwave in 30-second increments until chips just melt, stirring to combine between cook times. Allow to cool to 85°F. Remove eggs from refrigerator and dip one at a time in melted chocolate, then return to baking sheet. Allow to set at room temperature 30 minutes.

5. Drizzle eggs with white icing and finish with rainbow sprinkles. Serve immediately or refrigerate in an airtight container up to 6 days.

Bird of Paradise Refresher

Barcelona Lounge, Disney's Colorado Springs Resort, Easter

. . . ✦ . . .

The Barcelona Lounge sits waterfront on Lago Dorado at Disney's Coronado Springs Resort. Grab a Bird of Paradise Refresher and some appetizers while you enjoy the ambience of the area. If you are at home and/or in a place with dreary weather, whip up this beverage and feel its tropical flavors lift your spirits immediately. Easter is not only a religious holiday; it also recognizes the advent of spring, and this drink is a great way to welcome spring to your home: It tastes like paradise!

SERVES 1

8 ounces strawberry lemonade

1 ounce passion fruit juice

2 tablespoons passion fruit boba balls

In a 16-ounce plastic or glass cup, add strawberry lemonade and passion fruit juice and stir well to combine. Fill glass with ice and top with boba balls. Serve immediately.

Disney Parks Tip

Disney's Coronado Springs Resort added a new section in 2019, Gran Destino Tower, with luxurious rooms and access to all the amazing amenities of the Resort. Try staying there next time you visit central Florida!

Thumper Carrot Cakes

Various Resort Hotels, Easter

· · · ✦ · · ·

These cakes are very similar to a fan favorite served at Disney's Hollywood Studios all year round: the Carrot Cake Cookie. But this seasonal treat has the bonus of cute decor on top to celebrate Easter with everyone's favorite bunny, Thumper! Thumper is well-known from the classic Disney movie *Bambi*. And while this cake is served at many Resort Hotels across Walt Disney World in the spring, a great place to grab one is from Disney's All-Star Movies Resort, where you can dig in while admiring larger-than-life decor from the movies *Fantasia*, *Toy Story*, *101 Dalmatians*, *The Mighty Ducks*, and *The Love Bug*.

MAKES 6 CAKES

FOR CAKES

½ cup salted butter, softened
½ cup light brown sugar
½ cup granulated sugar
1 large egg
1 teaspoon vanilla extract
1¼ cups all-purpose flour
½ teaspoon baking powder
½ teaspoon baking soda
1 teaspoon ground cinnamon
½ teaspoon salt
½ cup old-fashioned rolled oats
½ cup unsweetened shredded coconut
½ cup chopped walnuts
2 large carrots, peeled and shredded

1. To make Cakes: Preheat oven to 350°F. Grease a twelve-divot whoopie pie pan with nonstick cooking spray and set aside.

2. In bowl of a stand mixer fitted with paddle attachment, cream together butter, brown sugar, and granulated sugar on low 2 minutes. Add egg and vanilla and beat to combine 2 minutes more. Gradually add flour ¼ cup at a time while continuing to mix until all flour is added. Add baking powder, baking soda, cinnamon, and salt and mix 1 minute more or until well combined.

3. In bowl of a food processor, add oats, coconut, and walnuts. Pulse until mix resembles coarse crumbs, about 2 minutes. Add to batter in stand mixer and mix 30 seconds to incorporate. Fold in shredded carrots.

(continued) ▶

FOR CREAM CHEESE FROSTING

- ½ cup salted butter, softened
- 4 cups confectioners' sugar
- 8 ounces cream cheese, softened
- 2 tablespoons heavy cream

FOR ASSEMBLY

- 6 tablespoons green frosting
- 6 sugar carrot decorations
- 6 teaspoons yellow frosting

4. Scoop batter into divots of prepared pan. Bake 12–15 minutes until a knife inserted comes out clean. Remove from oven and allow to cool completely in pan, about 45 minutes.

5. To make Cream Cheese Frosting: In a medium bowl, whisk together all ingredients. Scoop into a piping bag fitted with a medium round tip.

6. To Assemble: Flip 6 Cakes so flat side is facing up. Pipe Cream Cheese Frosting onto Cakes. Top Frosting with remaining 6 Cakes, with flat side down over Frosting. Pipe green frosting onto the top of each Cake to resemble grass, place a candy carrot piece on top of "grass," and next to candy carrot make a dollop of yellow frosting look like a tulip. Serve immediately or refrigerate in an airtight container up to 3 days.

Wookiee Cookies

· · · ✦ · · ·

Wookiee Cookies are a delicious and "chewy" homage to the Wookiee: a large, furry species of humanoid that is native to the forest planet of Kashyyyk. Wookiees, including copilot of the *Millennium Falcon* Chewbacca, are known for their strength, courage, and loyalty. Wookiee Cookies are a tasty way to celebrate this proud and noble species for May the Fourth (or whenever you choose).

MAKES 12 COOKIES

FOR COOKIES

12 teaspoons hazelnut-chocolate spread

1 cup salted butter, softened

1 cup light brown sugar

2/3 cup granulated sugar

2 large eggs

1 1/2 teaspoons vanilla paste

3 cups all-purpose flour

2 teaspoons cornstarch

1 teaspoon baking powder

1 teaspoon baking soda

1 teaspoon kosher salt

1 cup chocolate stick sprinkles

1. To make Cookies: Line a half-sized baking sheet with parchment paper. Scoop 12 1-teaspoon portions of hazelnut-chocolate spread onto parchment paper, making them as round as possible. Freeze to set at least 1 hour up to overnight.

2. Preheat oven to 375°F. Line two full baking sheets with parchment paper and set aside.

3. In bowl of a stand mixer fitted with paddle attachment, add butter, brown sugar, and granulated sugar and mix 2 minutes or until creamy. Add eggs and vanilla paste and mix 1 minute more. Slowly add in flour, cornstarch, baking powder, baking soda, and salt while mixer is running. Mix 1 minute or until combined.

4. Scoop cookie dough onto lined baking sheets using a 2-tablespoon cookie scoop to make 12 Cookies. Remove hazelnut-chocolate balls from freezer. Flatten cookie dough balls into pucks and wrap each hazelnut-chocolate ball completely in each cookie dough puck. Pour chocolate sprinkles into a shallow dish and roll cookie dough pucks in sprinkles. Set on prepared baking sheets, making sure each is given room to expand while baking.

FOR SASHES

1 cup milk chocolate
melting wafers

1 teaspoon fine silver
food shimmer dust

6 teaspoons chocolate
frosting

5. Bake one sheet at a time 12–15 minutes until bottom edges of Cookies turn golden brown. Allow to cool completely on sheets at least 1 hour.

6. To make Sashes: Pour chocolate wafers in medium microwave-safe bowl. Microwave on half power 30 seconds, stir, and microwave 30 seconds more. Repeat cooking and stirring until chocolate just melts. Pour melted chocolate onto a sheet of parchment paper and smooth in a single layer to about $\frac{1}{8}$" thickness. Allow to set in refrigerator about 30 minutes or until hard.

7. Cut hardened chocolate into $\frac{1}{2}$" × 3" rectangles. Use shimmer dust to paint tiny squares on each rectangle to mimic Chewbacca's sash. Use a dab of chocolate frosting to adhere each Sash to top of each Cookie. Serve immediately or store in an airtight container at room temperature up to 4 days.

Disney Parks Tip

Another version of this cookie is sold at Backlot Express in Disney's Hollywood Studios. Their version doesn't have sprinkles but does have a frosting filling between two oatmeal cookies. When you are visiting the Parks, try both and see which one you prefer!

Pride Artisan Marshmallows

Gasparilla's Island Grill, Disney's Grand Floridian Resort & Spa, Pride Month

· · · * · · ·

The rainbow or pride flag was designed back in 1978 by Gilbert Baker in San Francisco. He wanted to create a symbol that mimicked the American flag with its horizontal stripes. The colors most widely seen today each represent a deeper theme: red for life, orange for healing, yellow for sunlight, green for nature, blue for serenity, and purple for spirit. These six values embody the LGBTQIA+ movement. While this marshmallow recipe may be fluffy and cute, the colors are a beautiful reminder of those values.

SERVES 2

³⁄₄ cup water, divided

3 (0.25-ounce) packets unflavored gelatin

²⁄₃ cup light corn syrup

2 cups granulated sugar

1 teaspoon vanilla paste

4 drops each red, orange, yellow, green, blue, and purple gel food colorings

¹⁄₁₆ teaspoon each watermelon, blood orange, coconut, green apple, blue raspberry, and blueberry food flavorings

¹⁄₄ cup cornstarch

¹⁄₄ cup confectioners' sugar

1. Prepare six 4-ounce square plastic storage containers with a thin layer of nonstick cooking spray around entire interior of each. Set aside.

2. In bowl of a stand mixer fitted with whisk attachment, add ¹⁄₂ cup water, sprinkle gelatin on top of water, and let sit 5 minutes.

3. Combine remaining ¹⁄₄ cup water, corn syrup, granulated sugar, and vanilla paste in a small saucepan. Over medium heat, bring mixture to a boil and allow to boil 1 minute, stirring frequently.

4. Remove from heat and gently pour into stand mixer while mixing slowly until entire saucepan is emptied. Raise mixer speed to high and mix 12 minutes or until fluffy and stiff peaks form.

5. Evenly divide mixture into six small bowls. Dye each mixture with one gel food coloring color. Add more food coloring as necessary to make each color vivid. Add watermelon flavoring to red mixture, blood orange flavoring

to orange mixture, coconut flavoring to yellow mixture, green apple flavoring to green mixture, blue raspberry flavoring to blue mixture, and blueberry flavoring to purple mixture. Mix until colors and flavors are well incorporated. Scoop each bowl into one prepared square container. Grease six pieces of plastic wrap with nonstick cooking spray and smooth over top of each fluff. Allow to sit at room temperature 3 hours up to overnight.

6. Carefully slide each marshmallow out of its container and onto a cutting board. Use scissors greased with nonstick cooking spray to cut each color into two 2" × 2" × 1/2" rectangular marshmallows. Regrease scissors as needed. Eat or discard excess marshmallows.

7. Combine cornstarch and confectioners' sugar in a shallow bowl and roll each marshmallow in mixture, dusting off excess. Arrange marshmallows in two lines in order: red, orange, yellow, green, blue, purple. Serve immediately or store at room temperature in an airtight container up to 3 days.

Falling for Plant-Based

Various Resorts, Thanksgiving

· · · ✳ · · ·

Vegan lifestyles are becoming more common, with people choosing to tune in to the environment, sustainable practices, ethical sourcing, and their health. With this recipe, you can enjoy eating plant-based without sacrificing flavor. In fact, you may not even be able to tell these cupcakes are vegan! Many Resort Hotels carry this festive cupcake during the autumn months, but a fun place to grab one is from Landscape of Flavors at Disney's Art of Animation Resort. This Resort has samples of Disney artwork splashed across the walls in the restaurant and around the lobby.

SERVES 12

FOR CUPCAKES

1 cup granulated sugar
1 cup hot water
1/2 cup vegetable oil
1 tablespoon vanilla extract
1 tablespoon apple cider vinegar
1 1/2 cups gluten-free flour
1/2 cup unsweetened cocoa powder
1 teaspoon baking powder
1 teaspoon baking soda
1/2 teaspoon salt

1. To make Cupcakes: Preheat oven to 350°F. Insert paper cupcake liners into a twelve-divot muffin tin and set aside.

2. In bowl of a stand mixer fitted with paddle attachment, add sugar, hot water, oil, vanilla, and apple cider vinegar and mix on low until combined, about 2 minutes. Add in flour, cocoa, baking powder, baking soda, and salt and mix on low 2 more minutes or until no flour pockets remain.

3. Scoop batter evenly into cupcake liners and bake 18–20 minutes until a knife inserted comes out clean. Allow to cool in pan completely, about 45 minutes.

FOR VEGAN BUTTERCREAM

- **½ cup salted plant-based butter**
- **⅛ teaspoon salt**
- **2 cups powdered sugar**
- **⅓ cup unsweetened cocoa powder**
- **1½ teaspoons vanilla extract**
- **1 tablespoon plant-based milk**

FOR ASSEMBLY

- **12 tablespoons autumn-colored sprinkles**
- **12 tablespoons orange plant-based frosting**

4. To make Vegan Buttercream: In clean bowl of a stand mixer fitted with whisk attachment, add butter and salt and whisk until creamy, about 2 minutes. Gradually add in sugar, cocoa powder, vanilla, and milk on low speed until creamy and uniform. Scoop into a piping bag fitted with a star tip and refrigerate until ready to use.

5. To Assemble: Pipe Vegan Buttercream onto tops of Cupcakes and press autumn sprinkles into bottom ½" of Buttercream. Pipe orange frosting leaves onto Buttercream and serve immediately or refrigerate in an airtight container up to 3 days.

Pumpkin Pie Shake

Beaches & Cream Soda Shop, Disney Beach Club Resort, Thanksgiving

· · · ✦ · · ·

Beaches & Cream Soda Shop always knows how to take a milkshake and make it a spectacle, and this shake is no exception: It has a whole slice of pie on top! But no matter what pie you may choose to top this recipe, your friends and family will be gawking when you walk into Thanksgiving dinner with this in your hand. Beaches & Cream uses plastic jars for their shakes that you can take home, so if you get the chance to visit, buy a shake and keep the cup! For an extra-vibrant orange color, add a fourth drop of orange food coloring before blending.

SERVES 1

- 2 tablespoons caramel sauce
- 2 tablespoons vanilla frosting
- 2 tablespoons black and orange sprinkles
- 3 cups vanilla ice cream
- 1/4 cup whole milk
- 2 ounces salted caramel syrup
- 3 drops orange liquid food coloring
- 1/2 cup canned whipped cream
- 1 slice prepared pumpkin pie
- 2 milk chocolate candy melts

1. Prepare a pint Mason jar by drizzling caramel sauce inside. Spread frosting along outside of top rim and press sprinkles into frosting. Set aside.

2. In pitcher of a blender, add ice cream, milk, salted caramel syrup, and food coloring. Blend until smooth. Pour into prepared jar.

3. Top milkshake with a large dollop of whipped cream and place pumpkin pie on top of whipped cream. Finish with a small dollop of whipped cream on the pie slice and place milk chocolate candy melts on either side of whipped cream to resemble mouse ears. Add a large-gauge straw and serve immediately.

Cooking Hack

If you don't want to use store-bought pie for this recipe, simply make the Pumpkin Tart in this chapter and place one half of a Tart on top instead.

Butternut Squash Bisque

Grand Floridian Cafe, Grand Floridian Resort & Spa, Thanksgiving

· · · ✳ · · ·

Nothing hits quite like a warm bowl of homemade soup in the fall. It can warm you from the inside out and even brighten your spirits on a cold day. The Grand Floridian Resort & Spa is as impressive as the name suggests, but you don't need to have an overnight stay booked to eat at the Grand Floridian Cafe. Simply ride the Walt Disney World Monorail Resort Hotels line from the Transportation and Ticket Center and enjoy your Butternut Squash Bisque before whisking away to a day at Magic Kingdom.

SERVES 4

1 (12-ounce) bag frozen butternut squash chunks

3 tablespoons olive oil, divided

½ teaspoon chili powder

1 teaspoon garlic powder

1 teaspoon paprika

1 teaspoon salt

¼ teaspoon ground black pepper

1 medium yellow onion, peeled and diced

4 teaspoons minced garlic

¼ cup bourbon

2 cups vegetable stock

1 teaspoon vegetable bouillon paste

2 tablespoons pure maple syrup

¼ cup half-and-half

4 tablespoons toasted pepitas

1. Preheat oven to 450°F. Line a half-sized baking sheet with foil and set aside.

2. In a large bowl, toss butternut squash, 2 tablespoons olive oil, chili powder, garlic powder, paprika, salt, and pepper together. Pour onto baking sheet and spread into a single layer. Bake 18–20 minutes until fork-tender. Remove from oven and set aside.

3. In a large pot or Dutch oven, warm remaining 1 tablespoon olive oil over medium heat. Add onion and garlic and stir until onion is translucent and soft, about 4 minutes. Add bourbon to pan and stir. Add roasted butternut squash, vegetable stock, and bouillon paste. Stir until combined and allow to simmer 10 minutes.

4. Use an immersion blender or a stand blender in batches to blend and smooth soup into a purée.

5. Pour soup into four serving bowls. In a small bowl, combine maple syrup and half-and-half. Drizzle into soups and sprinkle with toasted pepitas. Serve immediately.

Pumpkin Tart

Various Resort Hotels, Thanksgiving

· · · ✳ · · ·

Pumpkin pie at Thanksgiving is almost as iconic as turkey. But unlike how turkey has many possible preparations (baked, smoked, deep-fried, sous vide, etc.) pumpkin pie usually looks about the same wherever you see it. Disney Resort Hotels wanted to maintain the classic taste of pumpkin pie while giving it a fresh and personalized feel. Enter the Pumpkin Tart: adorable little pies that you can eat all by yourself!

SERVES 4

1 (2-pack) refrigerated pie crust, room temperature

3/4 cup granulated sugar

2 1/2 teaspoons pumpkin pie spice

2 large eggs

1 (15-ounce) can pumpkin purée

1 (12-ounce) can evaporated milk

1 cup canned whipped cream

1. Preheat oven to 425°F. Gather four 4" tart pans.

2. Gently roll out pie crusts with a rolling pin. Cut 4 circles from dough using a 4" tart pan bottom as a guide. Place one dough circle in bottom of each of four 4" tart pans. Cut a 1" strip of dough to fit around circumference of each tart pan. Pinch strips to bottom circles in pans. Set aside.

3. In a large bowl, mix sugar, pumpkin pie spice, eggs, and pumpkin purée. Slowly add evaporated milk in a stream while continuing to stir. Stir until combined and wet. Carefully pour into prepared tart shells. Excess pie filling can be discarded or refrigerated in an airtight container up to 6 days.

4. Place tart pans on a half-sized baking sheet and bake 10–15 minutes until a knife inserted in center comes out clean. Remove from oven and allow to cool completely at room temperature, about 45 minutes, then refrigerate tarts 1 hour.

5. Once cooled, top each tart with a dollop of whipped cream and serve.

Millionaire Shortbread Bars

Centertown Market and Spyglass Grill, Disney's Caribbean Beach Resort, New Year's Eve

· · · ✳ · · ·

New Year's Eve parties are all about the glitz and glamour, so why not bring the money to your next NYE party with these Millionaire Shortbread Bars? Popular across Scotland for their decadence and deliciousness, millionaire shortbread is making its way across the globe and into everyone's kitchens. And while this recipe may appear daunting due to its many layers, each layer is simple to create. If you have a New Year's resolution to bake more, this is a great place to start!

SERVES 12

FOR LAYER ONE

1 cup salted butter, softened

½ cup granulated sugar

½ teaspoon salt

1 teaspoon vanilla extract

1 egg yolk

2 cups all-purpose flour

FOR LAYER TWO

½ cup salted butter, softened

1 cup light brown sugar

½ teaspoon salt

1 teaspoon vanilla extract

1 (14-ounce) can sweetened condensed milk

¼ cup light corn syrup

1. Preheat oven to 350°F. Line a 9" × 9" glass baking dish with parchment paper and set aside.

2. To make Layer One: In bowl of a stand mixer fitted with paddle attachment, cream together butter and sugar 1 minute on low speed. Add in salt, vanilla, and egg yolk and beat 1 minute more. Add in flour gradually while mixing until incorporated. Scoop into prepared pan and press into bottom. Use a fork to poke holes across dough. Bake 20–25 minutes until golden brown.

3. To make Layer Two: In a medium pot over medium heat, add butter, brown sugar, salt, vanilla, sweetened condensed milk, and corn syrup. Cook while continuing to stir frequently until a candy thermometer reads 225°F, 5–6 minutes. Pour over baked Layer One and smooth across surface. Refrigerate pan 10 minutes.

(continued) ▶

FOR LAYER THREE

$1\frac{1}{2}$ **cups semisweet chocolate chips**

$\frac{1}{4}$ **cup heavy whipping cream**

$\frac{1}{2}$ **cup slightly crushed pretzel pieces**

$\frac{1}{4}$ **cup crushed toffee pieces**

$\frac{1}{4}$ **cup gold sprinkles**

FOR ASSEMBLY

12 (.39" × .78") chocolate bar pieces

$\frac{1}{4}$ **cup white icing**

4. To make Layer Three: In a medium microwave-safe bowl, add chocolate chips and whipping cream. Microwave in 30-second increments, stirring in between, until just melted. Allow to cool to 85°F, then add pretzel and toffee pieces and fold to combine. Pour onto Layer Two in pan and smooth across surface. Top with sprinkles while still wet. Return to refrigerator to set 20 minutes.

5. To Assemble: Lift parchment paper out of pan and cut cooled contents into 12 rectangular bars. Place one chocolate bar piece flat side up on each bar and write new year date on chocolate using white icing. Serve immediately or store in an airtight container at room temperature up to 4 days.

Champagne Beignets

Scat Cat's Club—Lounge, Disney's Port Orleans Resort—French Quarter, New Year's Eve

· · · ✳ · · ·

Scat Cat's Club—Lounge serves beignets every day of the year, but the
Champagne Beignets are only served for *two days*: on December 31 and January 1.
Thanks to this recipe, you can enjoy the treat 365 days a year since no one needs an
excuse to pop open a bottle of bubbly. And if you don't have champagne lying around,
you can use any sparkling beverage to make the glaze.
Try using sparkling cider or even soda pop!

SERVES 10

FOR BEIGNETS

1½ cups warm water
   (110°F)

½ cup granulated sugar

1 (¼-ounce) packet
   active dry yeast

2 large eggs

1¼ teaspoons salt

1 cup evaporated milk

¼ cup shortening

7 cups bread flour

48 ounces vegetable oil,
   for frying

FOR CHAMPAGNE GLAZE

1 cup confectioners'
   sugar

2 tablespoons
   champagne

FOR ASSEMBLY

¼ cup iridescent
   sprinkles

1. To make Beignets: In a small bowl, stir water together with
   sugar and yeast. Let sit 10 minutes.

2. In bowl of a stand mixer fitted with paddle attachment, add
   eggs and beat 1 minute. Add salt and evaporated milk and
   beat 1 minute more. Add in yeast mixture and combine.
   Add shortening and mix 1 minute more. Gradually add in
   flour 1 cup at a time while continuing to mix on low until all
   flour is added. Switch to a dough hook and knead on low
   until dough comes together in a uniform mass, about
   5 minutes.

3. Grease a large bowl with nonstick cooking spray and place
   dough in bowl. Cover with greased plastic wrap and set
   in a warm place to rise, about 3 hours or until dough has
   doubled in size.

4. Pour oil into a large pot over medium heat and preheat
   to 350°F. Line a half-sized baking sheet with paper towels
   and set aside.

(continued) ▶

5. Flour a flat surface and roll dough out to ¼" thickness. Cut into Mickey shapes using a cookie cutter until all dough is cut.

6. Carefully slide 2 or 3 Mickey doughs into hot oil and fry about 1 minute on each side or until golden brown and cooked through. Remove to prepared baking sheet and repeat with remaining dough.

7. To make Champagne Glaze: In a small bowl, stir together sugar and champagne.

8. To Assemble: Place Beignets on serving plates. Drizzle with Champagne Glaze and top with iridescent sprinkles. Serve warm.

New Year's Float

Pineapple Lanai, Disney's Polynesian Village Resort, New Year's Eve

. . . ✦ . . .

Pineapple Lanai is always dishing up the best Dole Whip concoctions, and this float is no exception. The popping candy and boba balls are like New Year's fireworks popping and crackling in your mouth! For this recipe, you can make the Dole Whip and POG Juice ahead of time in bulk and allow your party guests to serve up their own floats while waiting for the countdown to the New Year.

SERVES 1

FOR DOLE WHIP

1 cup water
1½ cups granulated sugar
2 cups chilled pineapple juice
1 tablespoon lime juice

FOR POG JUICE

1 ounce passion fruit juice
2 ounces pulp-free orange juice
1 ounce guava juice

1. To make Dole Whip: In a medium microwave-safe bowl, combine water and sugar. Microwave 1 minute, stir, then microwave 1 minute more to create a syrup. Cover and refrigerate 2 hours.

2. Pour pineapple juice into ice cream machine and add ½ cup chilled syrup. Add lime juice and, following ice cream machine instructions, run about 20 minutes or until thick and creamy. Scoop into a piping bag fitted with a star tip and place in freezer until ready to use.

3. To make POG Juice: Add passion fruit, orange juice, and guava juice to a float glass and stir to combine.

(continued) ▶

FOR ASSEMBLY

1 tablespoon pineapple boba balls

1 tablespoon purple and red popping candy

4. To Assemble: Scoop boba balls into bottom of a 12-ounce float glass and pour in POG Juice. Pipe Dole Whip in a swirl on top of POG Juice. Top with popping candy and a drink umbrella. Serve immediately. Leftover syrup can be kept in the refrigerator up to 1 month, and leftover Dole Whip can be kept in the freezer up to 1 week.

Disney Parks Tip

If you're enjoying this treat at Pineapple Lanai, head over to the Polynesian Village Resort beach to view the fireworks at Magic Kingdom. They "pipe" the music from Main Street U.S.A. onto the beach so guests can enjoy all the fun from a different vantage point.

Standard US/Metric Measurement Conversions

VOLUME CONVERSIONS	
US Volume Measure	**Metric Equivalent**
⅛ teaspoon	0.5 milliliter
¼ teaspoon	1 milliliter
½ teaspoon	2 milliliters
1 teaspoon	5 milliliters
½ tablespoon	7 milliliters
1 tablespoon (3 teaspoons)	15 milliliters
2 tablespoons (1 fluid ounce)	30 milliliters
¼ cup (4 tablespoons)	60 milliliters
⅓ cup	90 milliliters
½ cup (4 fluid ounces)	125 milliliters
⅔ cup	160 milliliters
¾ cup (6 fluid ounces)	180 milliliters
1 cup (16 tablespoons)	250 milliliters
1 pint (2 cups)	500 milliliters
1 quart (4 cups)	1 liter (about)
WEIGHT CONVERSIONS	
US Weight Measure	**Metric Equivalent**
½ ounce	15 grams
1 ounce	30 grams
2 ounces	60 grams
3 ounces	85 grams
¼ pound (4 ounces)	115 grams
½ pound (8 ounces)	225 grams
¾ pound (12 ounces)	340 grams
1 pound (16 ounces)	454 grams

OVEN TEMPERATURE CONVERSIONS

Degrees Fahrenheit	Degrees Celsius
200 degrees F	95 degrees C
250 degrees F	120 degrees C
275 degrees F	135 degrees C
300 degrees F	150 degrees C
325 degrees F	160 degrees C
350 degrees F	180 degrees C
375 degrees F	190 degrees C
400 degrees F	205 degrees C
425 degrees F	220 degrees C
450 degrees F	230 degrees C

BAKING PAN SIZES

American	Metric
8 × 1½ inch round baking pan	20 × 4 cm cake tin
9 × 1½ inch round baking pan	23 × 3.5 cm cake tin
11 × 7 × 1½ inch baking pan	28 × 18 × 4 cm baking tin
13 × 9 × 2 inch baking pan	30 × 20 × 5 cm baking tin
2 quart rectangular baking dish	30 × 20 × 3 cm baking tin
15 × 10 × 2 inch baking pan	30 × 25 × 2 cm baking tin (Swiss roll tin)
9 inch pie plate	22 × 4 or 23 × 4 cm pie plate
7 or 8 inch springform pan	18 or 20 cm springform or loose bottom cake tin
9 × 5 × 3 inch loaf pan	23 × 13 × 7 cm or 2 lb narrow loaf or pâté tin
1½ quart casserole	1.5 liter casserole
2 quart casserole	2 liter casserole

General Index

261

*When a particular holiday rolls around, you'll be ready to flip to—and whip up—
the corresponding recipes in this book, thanks to the following index.
Here, all the recipes are organized by the holiday they celebrate!*

Index of Recipes by Holiday

About the Author

As a child who grew up in Anaheim Hills, California, Ashley Craft could recite the Star Tours ride by heart and navigate the Park without a map, and she fell asleep to the sound of Disneyland fireworks each night in her bedroom. After two internships at Walt Disney World and many, many more visits to the Disney Parks, Ashley is now one of the leading experts of

Disneyland and Walt Disney World. Her popular blog, *Unofficial Taste Tester*, is best known for featuring recipes inspired by Disney Parks foods to help people re-create that Disney magic right in their own kitchens. Her first book, *The Unofficial Disney Parks Cookbook*, became an instant bestseller. She lives in Minnesota with her husband, Danny; their children, Elliot, Hazel, and Clifford; and their cats, Figaro, Strider, and Kelpie. Follow her on *Instagram* at @UnofficialTasteTester.

TASTE *the* MAGIC *of* DISNEY!

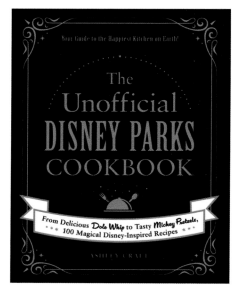

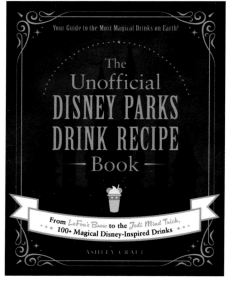

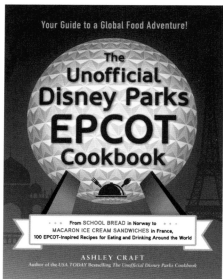

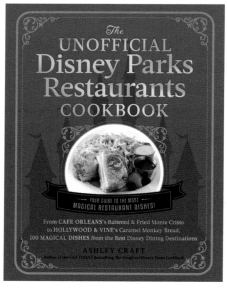

Pick Up or Download Your Copies Today!